MEN of STEEL

Vir Sanghvi is probably the best-known Indian journalist of his generation. Founder editor of *Bombay,* his career has included editorships of *Imprint, Sunday,* and then *Hindustan Times.*

Sanghvi also has a parallel career as an award-winning TV interviewer and has hosted various successful shows on the Star TV network and on the NDTV news channel. One of India's premier food writer, his book *Rude Food* won the Cointreau Award, the international food business's Oscar, for Best Food Literature Book in the world.

He is the author (along with Rudrangshu Mukherjee) of *India Then and Now,* also published by Roli Books.

MEN Of STEEL

India's Business Leaders in
Candid Conversations with Vir Sanghvi

LOTUS COLLECTION
ROLI BOOKS

Lotus Collection

© Vir Sanghvi, 2007

First published in 2007
This paperback edition first published in 2008
The Lotus Collection
An imprint of
Roli Books Pvt. Ltd.
M-75, G.K. II Market, New Delhi 110 048
Phones: ++91 (011) 2921 2271, 2921 2782
2921 0886, Fax: ++91 (011) 2921 7185
E-mail: roli@vsnl.com
Website: rolibooks.com
Also at
Varanasi, Bangalore, Chennai, Jaipur & Mumbai

Cover design: Sneha Pamneja
Layout design: Kumar Raman
Photographs Courtesy: HT Media Ltd.

ISBN: 978-81-7436-474-613-9
Rs. 95/-

Typeset in Minion by Roli Books Pvt. Ltd. and
printed at Anubha Printers, Noida (UP)

contents

MEN Of STEEL

Ratan Tata
Chairman, Tata Group

Nandan Nilekani
MD & CEO, Infosys

Azim Premji
Chairman & MD, Wipro Limited

Nusli Wadia
Chairman, Wadia Group of Companies

Bikki Oberoi
Vice Chairman & MD, East India Hotels

Subhash Chandra
Chairman, Zee Telefilms and Essel Group

Kumar Mangalam Birla
Chairman, Aditya Birla Group

Vijay Mallya
Chairman, UB Group

Sunil Bharati Mittal
Chairman & MD, Bharti Group

Rajeev Chandrasekhar
Former Chairman & CEO, BPL Mobile

Uday Kotak
Vice Chairman & MD,
Kotak Group of Companies

introduction

▲

The profiles contained in this book were never intended to be part of a series. It was the first one that I wrote that led to all the others.

It happened this way. I had been planning to interview Ratan Tata for a year before we actually sat down for a meeting. Somehow his dates never matched mine. Whenever I was in Mumbai, he would be travelling. And when he was in Delhi, he was always too busy.

Then, three days before we launched the Mumbai edition of the *Hindustan Times*, Ratan found a window in his schedule. He was in Delhi for half a day and could spare an hour if I was willing to come to his suite at the Taj.

Naturally, I grabbed the opportunity.

At the best of times, Ratan is a shy, reticent man who is always uncomfortable talking about himself. Ask him about Tata Steel's productivity and he will have all the figures at his fingertips. Push him about his plans for the Indica and he will suddenly come to life. But no sooner do you begin discussing the ouster of Rusi Mody than an invisible veil descends over his face and the answers become strained and monosyllabic.

Well, I guess I was lucky. For some reason, Ratan seemed ready to talk. We discussed all the things that people said about him – but which he never publicly acknowledged. Did it hurt him that so many critics had seen him as an essentially mediocre man who had been catapulted to the top of Tata Sons only because of his surname? How did he feel about ousting so many of the top managers to whom J.R.D. Tata had handed over control of the Tata empire? And, was he a lonely man who was unable to make friends?

I have never worked out why Ratan agreed to discuss the issues he had spent the last decade avoiding in every media interaction. Perhaps I got him when he was in a reflective mood. Or maybe enough time had now elapsed for him to be able to talk dispassionately about the events that shaped his career.

We spend more than the allotted hour and when the interview ended, I was faced with a dilemma. If I wrote it up in a straightforward question-and-answer format, I worried that I would lose the nuances. But did I know enough about him to write a profile?

In the event, I decided that it would work best as a straight piece of 2,000 words – about four times the size of the average newspaper article – and quickly commandeered a full-page of the first issue of the Mumbai edition (sometimes, it helps to be the boss) to run the profile.

Though the *HT* was launched in Mumbai with a high-profile crime story (about Salman Khan and the underworld) that dominated TV news for many days afterwards, I was surprised to find that many readers remembered the Ratan Tata profile. It had given them an insight into the man behind the corporate results, they said.

Writers are rarely humble about their own work. And though I was proud of the piece, I was realistic enough to realize that the praise was not directed at the quality of my journalism but sprang from an appreciation of the format.

Businessmen are usually profiled by business journalists. They ask them questions about price-to-earnings ratios and discuss group turnover. The interviewees are happy with this format. Some hapless PR hack has probably briefed them about the likely questions before the interview and so, the responses are ready and rehearsed.

Rarely, if ever, does the real person break through the figures. Other businessmen read the interviews and profiles and find them fascinating. The rest of us read the first paragraph and then turn the page.

The Ratan Tata piece, I guessed, had worked because I am not a business journalist. Each time I read a story in the business papers, my eyes glaze over when it comes to the figures. My approach had been to treat Ratan as I would have treated anybody else I had interviewed: a politician, a film star, an author, or whatever.

It was a format that could work, I decided. And so, every Monday I commandeered the same full page of the Mumbai edition (the vast majority of the profiles never appeared in Delhi) to devote 2,000 words to one of India's top industrialists.

It was surprisingly easy to get the businessmen to talk. I bumped into Subhash Chandra on a flight and he was kind enough to drop in at my hotel in Mumbai the next evening for a drink and a chat. Nusli Wadia invited me home for dinner and we spoke late into the night. Nandan Nilekani and I spent hours at a coffee lounge in a Delhi hotel talking about the old days. Azim Premji spoke to me over lunch at his office in Bangalore. Rajeev Chandrasekhar spent a day with me during which we managed to have a fairly liquid dinner.

Some were more difficult. Kumar Birla presented a special sort of problem. He is not keen on personal interviews. And besides, there were the questions of conflict of interest. I work for the *Hindustan Times*, which is largely owned by another branch of the Birla family. Should we be profiling a Birla?

Eventually, I decided that it made no sense to exclude one of India's top industrialists only because he was related to the chairman of the *Hindustan Times*. But that still left me with the problem of getting him to talk. Finally, my boss Shobhana Bhartia, who is Kumar's aunt, phoned him and fixed the interview. So, the Birla connection did help.

There are two notable exceptions in the list of profiles. Neither Ambani brother features. Ironically, these were the two profiles I was best equipped to have written because I have known both Mukesh and Anil ever since they returned to India from university in America and joined the family business.

Neither actually refused to be interviewed but they both made the same stipulation. They would talk about everything except for each other. At the time, the Ambani-split was dominating headlines. It made no sense to write profiles of either man without recording his views on the circumstances that led to the bitter parting. So, I regretfully decided to exclude the brothers from the list.

Have the profiles dated since they were written? In some sense, I suppose they have. Business is a constantly changing activity. I interviewed Rajeev Chandrasekhar just after he'd sold his stake in BPL Mobile. Presumably, he will start something new in the months ahead. And so, the profile will be out of date in that it does not capture the full extent of his business activities.

But I doubt very much if Rajeev will change a great deal as a person, no matter what his choice of new venture is. The point of these profiles is that they are less about facts and figures, profit and loss, and price and earnings; more about the men themselves and the circumstances that shaped their destinies. In that sense, at least, I don't think the profiles will date.

India is a society in ferment, Indian business is constantly transforming itself. So it is possible that these men will not remain at the top of their fields forever. But I chose them quite carefully. And I am willing to bet that for the next decade or so, these will still be the top names of Indian business.

Delhi, July 2006

Vir Sanghvi

nandan nilekani
MD & CEO, Infosys

▲

've known Nandan Nilekani for over twenty-five years now. Or, to put it differently, for half of his life. When we first met in Mumbai in 1980, he was two years out of IIT, worked for a computer firm called Patni Associates in Nariman Point and none of us, Nandan included, had the slightest idea that he would become a household name by the end of the century. Or that he would be worth in excess of Rs 3,000 crore.

In that more modest era, Nandan's salary was a princely Rs 1,200 a month. And he thought he was making good money. After all, when his father retired, the old man's salary was Rs 1,200. As Nandan now recalls, ' It seemed like a very good deal to start your career with a salary that was the same as your father's at the end of his career.'

The figures should tell you something about Nandan's background: solid, well-educated, South Indian middle-class Brahmin. But they also reveal that he came from a family that never had much money. But never minded that it wasn't rich.

By most standards, Nandan's climb to wealth and fame is an astonishing success story. And yet, in the context of the Indian IT business, it is not that unusual. Admittedly, few techies have been

[
'What was Infosys? It was an idea.
What do we owe our success to?
To ideas, not to labour and machinery.'
]

as successful as Nandan. But there's no shortage of success stories nevertheless. And most of the new billionaires started out as well-educated middle to lower-middle-class South Indian boys.

So, I'm not that surprised that an old friend from all those years ago is now so rich. Or, that the once anonymous engineer is now so widely recognized: throughout our interview, everybody else in the coffee shop where we are chatting, stops to gawk at him.

No, my astonishment is about the manner in which Nandan has transformed his personality.

In the 'On' mode always

My first impression of Nandan, and one that endured for nearly two decades was: there's more to this man than meets the eye.

He did not say much, never spoke about himself and deflected all serious questions with an easy laugh. But even when he was not participating in a conversation, you always had a sense that he was watching closely. Even when everybody else had drunk themselves silly and Nandan appeared to be asleep and totally out of it, I always knew that he was fully alert.

This was a man who was never Off. No matter how laidback he seemed, he was always On.

Now, a quarter century after we first met, I finally confront him with this perception. Was it not true, I ask, that he prided himself on an alert detachment? That he would be part of every situation and yet not be part of it; that, at some level, he would always be an observer, watching with a dispassionate interest?

Nandan Nilekani smiles. 'Yes that's true,' he says. 'I was always very detached.'

But that, I say, is the real change. Despite the millions, he is still recognizably the Nandan of old. The difference is in the manner. He is now much more willing to give of himself. He has lost that old dispassionate detachment. You now feel that you know what he thinks. A certain passion seems to emanate from the core of his being. Ask him a question, and he will give you a straight answer. There won't be the jokey deflections of old.

'That's deliberate,' Nandan says finally.

Deliberate? Did he just get up one morning and say to himself, I must be less zipped up?

'I was told,' he explains, 'that my approach to life was too cerebral. I was told that I was too much of an observer. If I was going to lead an organization then I needed to show passion. I needed to allow people to connect with me.'

So, was it just a business decision?

'No, I think I've changed as a person. I am more willing to engage. I feel more passionately about things. And I'm able to be much more demonstrative than I ever thought was possible.'

And is he happier this way?

He laughs. 'Yes, of course. Doesn't it show?'

It does.

A meeting that changed his life

Nandan Nilekani is clear that he does not owe his current position or prominence to his brains. Yes, of course, he was bright. He came first in school when he was at Bishop Cotton in Bangalore. At the age of twelve, he went to live with an uncle in Dharwad and spent four years at Karnataka College in that town before finally getting into IIT, Mumbai.

'I had always been in the top three in my class at school. But getting into IIT was a revelation. I studied electrical engineering, which was then the most popular course, so we had some of the brightest minds in IIT. And compared to those guys, I was not outstanding. I was never at the top of my class. There were people who were just so much brighter than me.'

For Nandan, the real breakthrough at IIT was social. He says he spent four years away from his parents. He has never lived at his parental home since the age of twelve because it was felt that his father would travel around and the young Nandan would have a more stable childhood with his uncle in Dharwad.

This had two immediate consequences. The first was that he developed what he now describes as a sense of independence at a young age; psychologists will probably trace the roots of his cerebral detachment to this phase. The second was that the shift from Dharwad to Mumbai was traumatic in class terms.

'In those days,' he remembers, 'a very different kind of person went to IITs. It was all sophisticated big city guys from places like Cathedral School. They had never met anybody who had gone to school in Dharwad.'

He says that the early years were difficult in social terms but that he worked on what he quickly identified as one of his core strengths: his organizational skills. 'I realized that I was good at organizing things. So I got involved in organizing *Mood Indigo* and other such events. I became a quizzer, and in my final year I was the general secretary of IIT Mumbai.'

By the end of 1978, when his engineering term was coming to an end, Nandan rejected the standard find-a-job-abroad option because of what he now describes as 'inertia and laziness'. He considered applying for an MBA course but even that fell through when he was taken ill before the IIM entrance exam.

So he looked for a job in Mumbai, joined Patni Systems, and met N.R. Narayan Murthy.

And his life changed forever.

A walk-out called Infosys

The history of global business is replete with stories of *guru-chela* relationships (what they describe as 'mentoring' in the text books) but I know of no other Indian company where a relationship between a genius and his protégé has led to such happy consequences.

In the late 1970s, Narayan Murthy headed a division for the Patnis, evolved a relationship with one of the Patni brothers and was left pretty much on his own.

Murthy had his own approach to hiring. He preferred young people straight out of college to engineers with experience. But he didn't trust exam results alone. So when Nandan went for his interview, he was startled to find that Murthy expected him to solve puzzles and behaved like a schoolmaster conducting an IQ test.

Obviously, Nandan was good at puzzles because Murthy hired him on the spot and the two men quickly became close. But, insists Nandan, he was not the only young man whom Murthy mentored: 'He has extraordinary leadership qualities and the entire division hero-worshipped him.'

In 1981, the Patni brother who normally interacted with Murthy was out of town and another brother treated him roughly. Nandan refuses to divulge details of the disagreement but from what I remember of that era, it went like this: Murthy was asked to do something he disagreed with; he asked Mr Patni for an explanation and was told '*tum apna kaam karo*, just do what you're told to do.'

Anyone who has met Murthy will recognize that he places self-respect above everything else. So naturally, he walked out. And naturally, his entire division walked out with him.

They were fed up of working for traditional bania bosses, they said. They would launch their own company.

That company was, of course, Infosys.

The Punjabi who missed it

The origins of Infosys have now become the stuff of business legend but I suspect the story has been somewhat sanitized in the retelling.

From what I remember, the guiding motive may well have been to create an ethical, professionally-managed company, as Murthy and Nandan declare in all their interviews to the pink papers, but the phrase they used in those days, has been airbrushed out of the history.

They wanted, they said, to create an 'un-Marwari company'.

By this they meant – or so I understood at the time – that they wanted to run Infosys as the antithesis of the typical Marwari-bania business of that era. Employees would be treated with respect. No bribes would be paid. There would be no cash transactions. Nobody would take any money out of the company. And all decisions would be taken by a professional collective, not by sethji and his sons.

Nandan now professes memory loss when confronted with the phrase 'the un-Marwari company', but I'm pretty sure that this is how Murthy and his colleagues saw Infosys in those days.

Of the defectors from Patni Systems, there were six South Indians, including Nandan and Murthy, and one Punjabi, Ashok Arora.

Nandan bristles at the suggestion that Infosys represented the revolt of South Indian Brahmins against the North Indian banias who dominated Indian business at the time. 'South Indians are not a monolith,' he says. 'Three of us were from Karnataka, two from Kerala, one from Tamil Nadu and anyway, Ashok Arora was a Punjabi.'

All of which is undoubtedly true. And it is also true that of the six South Indians, one was a non-Brahmin.

But it is as true that Ashok Arora did not stay the course, leaving Infosys much before it hit the big time.

Had he hung on, he would be a billionaire today.

Infosys goes Public ... and it's the FIIs

In the early years, Infosys followed a travelling model. Murthy stayed on in India while his protégés went off to foreign countries to work onsite for a variety of clients. In July 1981, Nandan went to the US and though he came back to Bangalore for a few months in 1984, he spent much of that decade in America.

Though the company did reasonably well, it never made big money. And whatever it did earn was reinvested into the business while the partners took the smallest salaries possible.

My recollections are hazy but I seem to recall that there was even some talk of dissolving the business in the late 1980s and that only the force of Murthy's personality – along with Nandan's conviction that the company would make it – kept Infosys going.

Things changed for the better with the economic reforms – Murthy is on record as saying that Infosys owes its success to Manmohan Singh's liberalization – and in 1991, the company suddenly began to look like a winner. The turnover demonstrates that trend. In 1991, the figure was Rs 5.5 crore; by 1992 it was 9.5 crore; by 1993 it was 14 crore; by 1994 it was 30 crore till it reached 509 crore by 1999.

Nandan says that they were in the right place at the right time. In 1991, foreign companies began looking at India as a base for software operations, the reforms made the country seem attractive to global investors and the government introduced a policy to jumpstart software exports.

Even so, when Infosys went public in 1993, many of the early investors tended to be foreign institutions that recognized the potential of the software sector. Indian investors were leery of investing in a business that had no labour force, no plant and no machinery.

I suppose I was one of the sceptics. When Nandan urged me to buy Infosys shares at the time of the public issue, I had never bought stocks in my life and even an investment of Rs 10,000 seemed like a huge sacrifice.

It was not, as Nandan sometimes jokingly suggests, that I was unwilling to invest in a company part owned by an old friend whose own salary had not been more than a few thousand rupees for most of the 1980s and who only bought his first car at the end of the decade.

It was more that, like the rest of the Indian middle class, I had been taken by surprise by the forces unleashed by liberalization and by the technological revolution.

But Nandan knew what was going on. He knew what the future would look like. And he knew how Infosys would ride the boom.

(For the record, I am told that Rs 10,000 invested in Infosys in 1993 would be worth over a crore today. So now you know why he's so rich and I'm so poor).

Money matters

The rest of the Infosys story is well known. As profits rose, it quickly became, along with the Tatas, the most admired company in India. Its success became a byword for Indian ingenuity and proof that Indians could compete in the global market.

Today, it is the fourth largest company in India in terms of market capitalization, way ahead of Tata Steel, Tata Motors, BHEL, L&T, State Bank of India, ITC and, since the founders were so keen on this bigger than any Marwari company. (For the record, the three companies that are larger are ONGC, NTPC and Reliance).

A few years ago, Murthy announced that he would step back from the actual running of the company. Another of the founders, N.S. Raghavan said that the company needed a younger man to manage it and the collective that makes the decisions at Infosys (in the manner of a politburo) chose Nandan to be the chief executive.

Murthy is still around, of course, but his new designation, Chief Mentor, captures his real strength. Nandan rates him as one of the top five businessmen in Indian history, 'along with J.R.D. Tata, G.D. Birla, Dhirubhai Ambani and ... well, I don't know ... there must be somebody else.'

Nandan is absurdly rich. His personal wealth fluctuates with the share price but the figure is usually in excess of Rs 3,000 crore. The founders pay themselves relatively modest salaries – Nandan was paid Rs 40 lakh last year – and bill no expenses to the company. Murthy has turned travelling economy class and refusing to stay in five-star hotels into something of an Infosys fetish but his colleagues seem to share his asceticism with varying degrees of enthusiasm.

Nandan's own income, of course, has nothing to do with his salary. Over the last four years, his family has received Rs 66 crore as dividends. Plus there's the Rs 392 crore from sale of shares through two ADR offerings.

How does he feel about the money?

'It's crazy,' he laughs. 'It's a joke.'

IT for the people

So what does Nandan Nilekani do with his crores when he's not laughing over them?

The raison d'être of Infosys has always been to do things differently. Murthy treats his success as proof that it is possible to be honest and still prosper in India. (Yeah, sure, say the sceptics, but only if all your customers are foreign companies, you don't have any factories, don't have to pay sales tax or excise and you don't need any government permissions.) Murthy has set new standards for corporate governance and is something of a messiah for the Indian middle class, demonstrating that it is the values of the educated Indian professional that will bring us global success, not the values of the bania business class, cosseted and protected during the licence-permit raj.

Nandan is less judgemental but determined to make a difference to society outside of the purview of Infosys. He was actively involved with a scheme to help solve Bangalore's civic problems and has offered to provide technological solutions, at his own cost, to any major Indian city that is looking for them. He's offering systems to Delhi to allow greater transparency in governance.

Though he is reluctant to talk about this, the answer to the question of what he does with his money is simple enough: he gives most of it away. Along with his wife Rohini, he spends crores each year on philanthropic activities. When Rohini earned Rs 100 crore from Infosys' ADR issue (she was one of the first shareholders in the company) she put it into an educational foundation she runs.

Nandan offers two justifications. The first is the great wealth-great responsibility argument. He has made his money, he says, by being in the right place at the right time. There are people who are much brighter than him and who work much harder. His wealth is partly a consequence of good timing. In such circumstances, he has an obligation to give it back to society. Not only is this a moral imperative but it is also practical: in a poor country like India, it would be obscene, he says, for an individual to make so much money and not want to share it with everyone else.

The second justification is even more practical. 'I really don't have many expensive tastes. I have more money than I will ever need. My children will not join the company and I believe in the middle-class tradition that they should earn a living themselves.'

He pauses. 'So what am I going to do with the money? Leave it to charity when I die? In that case, why not use it to do some good while I'm alive?'

The spreading of an idea

Nandan Nilekani has a new claim to fame these days. In a conversation with the American journalist Thomas Friedman, he remarked that the technological revolution had made the world a more equal, more even place. Friedman used many of Nandan's ideas – taking care to credit them to the source – in his book, *The World is Flat*.

That book has been an extraordinary success, topping best-seller lists in the US and selling 800,000 copies to date. Even the title comes from Nandan's contention about evening the playing field.

How does it feel, I ask him, to know that his ideas are reaching Americans who've never heard of him or of Infosys?

'It's a great feeling. It's actually the best feeling,' he says honestly. 'That's the kind of thing I really enjoy. What was Infosys? It was an idea. What do we owe our success to? To ideas, not to labour and machinery. And now I find that my ideas are influencing people I have never met. How can I not enjoy that?'

So is there a cerebral satisfaction in that?

'Yes, it's cerebral,' he stops to think. 'But it's also a passion. So you see, I have changed. I'm not just cerebral. I'm passionate too.'

Nandan Nilekani laughs softly to himself.

kumar mangalam birla

Chairman, Aditya Birla Group

▲

Before we go any further, I have to declare an interest. The *Hindustan Times* is part of the K.K. Birla Group and Kumar Mangalam Birla is K.K. Birla's grandnephew. Both men run their businesses separately and Kumar has nothing at all to do with the way in which the *HT* is run. But still there is a family connection and I think it's only fair to mention this straight out.

As far as I am concerned, there is also a second connection. Both Kumar and I are on the board of governors of the Birla Institute of Technology and Science (BITS) in Pilani. I was invited to join the board before the *HT* hired me and before Kumar became its governor, but for what it's worth, we do occupy places on the same board.

The point of the BITS connection is that it offered me a chance to see how people view Kumar. I had first met him some years before he turned up at the board meeting (I had also interviewed him on TV many years ago), but many of the others at the meeting – faculty, alumni, etc. – had never been in the same room as him before.

When the chairman introduced him as a new governor, there were audible gasps from some of the alumni. 'Is he the Kumar

[
' ... A brand is not about individuals,
whatever it stands for is really a tribute
to the team we have created ... '
]

Birla?' somebody asked. And afterwards, people lined up to shake his hand.

In Mumbai for this interview, two years after that board meeting, I remind Kumar of the manner in which he was treated by the BITS people. Was he surprised or embarrassed or flattered by the reaction? After all, there are not many businessmen who would evoke this kind of response.

I don't remember how embarrassed Kumar seemed then but today he blushes a deep red and seems decidedly awkward. 'Come on, it wasn't like that,' he protests feebly.

But, of course, it was. I remember the incident only too well, I tell him.

Besides, is it not true that when he goes to address functions at management institutes, he ends up signing dozens of autographs and having to pose for photographs with the students?

Kumar Birla now looks very embarrassed.

Finally, he comes up with an explanation. 'I don't remember the BITS incident,' he says, 'but I suppose that management students and young managers probably look up to me a little bit. But for the world at large, I don't think I am anybody special. I don't think anyone even recognizes me. I think I am quite anonymous.'

Oh really?

Driven by passion

Several years ago when I interviewed Kumar for Star TV, he was already well known. He had appeared on Simi Garewal's programme, *Rendezvous with Simi Garewal*, and had been profiled extensively in the non-business press.

Despite that, he was extraordinarily diffident. For fifteen minutes before we shot the first segment, he kept saying things like 'what is there to ask me?' Then, during the first break, he looked perturbed. 'This is so boring,' he said. I persevered and finished the interview.

That wasn't so bad, I said, finally.

'Well, I thought it was very boring,' he said. 'Can we do it again?'

And so, we re-shot the first two segments.

I didn't think there was much difference between the first shoot and the re-shoots, but Kumar reckoned that he was much more relaxed the second time around. Even so, when the interview was finally over, he was back to saying things like 'I don't know why you are interviewing me. Your guests are usually so interesting. I really don't have anything to say.'

I remind him of the shoot and the re-shoots. Does he still think he is boring? I ask.

'No, I don't think I am boring,' he says with a surprising firmness. 'I don't think I am boring at all.'

Does this mean that he has grown more interesting in the intervening period? Or has he just grown in confidence?

Neither, apparently. 'I never thought I was boring,' says he.

And the re-shoots?

'I just wasn't sure that people would be that interested in me.'

Make what you will of that distinction but Kumar is clear about what is boring and what is not. 'I admit that I used to be petrified of TV,' he concedes, 'but I am very passionate about what I do. And I don't think passion can ever be boring. I find anybody who has a passion – even if he is single-minded about that one passion – very interesting. So I don't know why you got the impression that I thought I was boring.'

GenNext icon

Even if Kumar Birla had been a mediocre businessman, he would still be one of the big hitters of Indian industry. His father, Aditya Birla, was probably the greatest businessman of his generation, a true visionary who had the foresight and wisdom to professionalize his group and look for opportunities abroad. When Aditya died in 1995, the group was already worth Rs 8,000 crore.

If Kumar had been content to manage the businesses that his father left him, and had not bothered with acquisitions or new projects, he would probably be sitting on a group that was worth around Rs 12,000 crore merely on the basis of normal growth. At that level, he would have been one of the country's leading businessmen.

Except, of course, that Kumar has not been content to just manage the legacy. He has transformed his father's empire, turned many of its business practices inside out and today his group has a market cap of over Rs 34,000 crore.

And he is just thirty-eight years old.

Nobody I know is willing to predict what size his group will be by the time Kumar is fifty. Of one thing, however, everybody I speak to is absolutely sure: like his father before him, Kumar is the outstanding businessman of his generation.

Transforming the legacy

It needn't necessarily have turned out that way. In 1995, when Aditya Birla died at the age of fifty-two, many people were not sure how the empire would fare without his masterly touch.

At the time, Kumar was only twenty-eight and, by common consent, too young to fill the shoes of India's greatest businessman. Moreover, Aditya was a charismatic figure and many of his senior managers were emotionally committed to his memory. 'I remember that for the first few months there would be times when somebody would mention my father during a meeting and we would have senior executives bursting into tears and leaving the room,' says Kumar.

Many of these executives had known Kumar as a child and he felt awkward telling them what to do, or holding them accountable for their performance. Plus, there was his own sense that India was changing more rapidly than most people realized. In 1991, Manmohan Singh had begun the liberalization process and many of the old cosy certainties that traditional families like the Birlas had grown up with were vanishing.

'I knew that we needed a transformation,' Kumar recalls. 'Not a cosmetic transformation but a fundamental change in the way in which we did things. My only question was: when? I was never sure whether I needed to wait before making the changes that I thought were necessary. The timing needed to be worked out carefully.'

Eventually, of course, he found the right time. In the Birla Group, there was a womb-to-tomb policy. People rarely retired. And it was assumed that their children had guaranteed jobs with the group.

Kumar changed all that. 'I felt that if people never retired, then there was no place for younger people to rise. So it was important to institute a retirement policy,' he says. In real terms, this involved retiring 350 employees over the age of sixty. As for the guaranteed jobs for family members, his view was 'what used to happen was that if one son was very bright, he went to work for a multinational. The other son, if he wasn't good enough for anywhere else, was sent off to work for us. So I instituted a policy that vetted all applications from family members of existing employees. None of this made me very popular but I thought it needed to be done and now, I think people are much more accepting of the policy.'

My father, my hero

Did it require guts to chart out his own course? To reverse policies set in motion by G.D. Birla and carried through by B.K. Birla and Aditya Birla?

'It's an interesting thing about my family,' says Kumar, 'that while my elders were very conscious of certain values, they always encouraged us to make our own business decisions.'

What kind of values?

'Simple things. The Birlas are very conscious about punctuality. We are not ostentatious. We have a great sense of family. I remember that during my vacations I would always go off to Calcutta to be with my grandparents. We are taught to respect older people. Good manners and regard for other people are considered very important.'

Did he have much to do with G.D. Birla?

'I was fifteen when he passed away so I have quite clear memories of him. He would take a great interest in the little things that mattered to me. If I had an exam, then no matter where he was, he would phone and ask me how I had done. If I told him I was not going to have dinner because I was going out, he would want to know where I was going. If I said I was going to Sardar's, he would want to know what that was, what pav bhaji was, that sort of thing.'

What about his own father?

'I hero-worshipped him. Even though he was a very busy man and travelled a great deal, he was always there when I needed him. He came to my every school function. He always made time for me. He knew who my friends were, he knew what I was doing. And because he was so good with people, he always knew how to get the best out of me. He could be tough as knuckles but he was tactful about it. He could be threatening, cajoling, soft, depending on what he thought I would respond to.'

Was there a lot of pressure to live up to the legacy?

'In some ways, I was brought up in a pressure-cooker environment. Though I was very close to my father and there was a strong bonding, I was also scared of him. But I trusted him implicitly. If he said something was right for me, I always did it. I remember when I had finished my ICSE, he phoned me and said that he had thought I should do my chartered accountancy simultaneously while I was doing my B.Com. The exam was only two weeks away and all my friends thought I was crazy. And yes, it was work, work, and work. But I trusted my father's judgement and it never even occurred to me to say no.'

Did he realize quite how obsessed his father was with him?

'No, why do you say that?'

I tell him about the time I interviewed Aditya Birla in 1980 (or perhaps it was 1981) and he talked with great emotion about the time his son Kumar had fallen ill. The boy was ten and the prognosis was not good. He had meningitis and the doctors were not sure if he would survive.

Aditya gave up his business, stopped going to office and sat every day by his son's bedside for nearly two months. 'I said to myself that money, business, nothing else matters, I just want my son to get well,' Aditya had recalled in his interview to me. He even took up painting as a means of relaxing and taking his mind off his son's health during this period.

Kumar has very vague memories of his illness. He says that he knows how his father reacted only because he had told him about it when he was older. But at the time, he had no understanding of how serious the illness was and how worried the family was.

'You know what it is like with kids,' he smiles. 'All I remember is that I missed school for two months.' A pause. 'But I still topped my class that year.' Charting a new path, Kumar says that he got involved in some small way in the family business when he was fifteen. 'I remember being tutored by my father, sitting in on meetings and asking him questions afterwards. Later, I looked after the cement business of Grasim and got involved in Indo-Gulf.

'I was always taught to be independent. My father, my grandfather and my great-grandfather always made it clear to me that when it came to business, I had to take my own decisions and then take responsibility for them. Nobody tried to force me to do anything or made my decisions for me. At the time, this was tough but later, it stood me in good stead.'

Kumar went off to London to study for an MBA when he was just twenty-two, even though most of the other people in his class were twenty-nine. When he came back, he was uniquely qualified because he had studied chartered accountancy, had a commerce degree and an MBA. Plus, he had been tutored by the master: Aditya Birla.

Did anybody have any inkling, I wonder, that he would be pushed into the driving seat so soon?

'No, we found out that my father was ill about two years before he passed away. And though nobody said anything in so many words, I felt that once he knew, he made a conscious attempt to fast-track me in a very matter-of-fact sort of way,' he says. 'But I'll tell you something: even though we knew how unwell he was, it never ever occurred to me that there would be a time when he wouldn't be here with us.'

Never? Even though he knew his father had cancer?

'No, never. I met my father on the morning of the day he passed away. And I had no idea that by the end of the day he would not be there. It just never entered my mind.'

Later, when he was making all those changes in the way the group was run, did he wonder how his father would have reacted?

'I think many of the changes were a response to the changed environment. But I was always brought up to make my own decisions. I was never required to think "what would my father do?" As much as I hero-worshipped him, we have different styles.'

Such as?

'I think he was more hands-on. My style is much more to give people freedom to do their own thing. As long as they deliver, I don't like to get involved. They should have the freedom to do what they think necessary. I am available if they need me and I will hold them accountable but I will not interfere needlessly.'

Wasn't this a huge change for the group?

'Yes, it was. People used to say that when Aditya babu phoned somebody, that person would stand up while answering the phone. He was great at bilateral motivation and contact. My style is more group-oriented. I like motivating groups of people. I find that in business, it is more important to empower a whole group than to depend on a single individual. So in that sense, my approach is less bound by the baggage of tradition.'

He has done things that the Birlas have rarely done before. He has grown, for instance, through acquisition, a change of approach for the family. He has branched out into consumer products while the family fortune has really been founded on commodities.

'Yes, that's true. We still have a very strong presence in the commodities sector and I am very comfortable with that. But I see our group as a conglomerate. I am not a great believer in core competence. I am quite happy being involved in a variety of businesses, provided I am sure that we can attain a dominant position in those businesses. So you'll find us now in mutual funds, insurance and branded garments. In fact, we're the market leaders in the branded garment business.'

Passion is the key

The other thing he's done, of course, is that he's created a brand within a brand. Every Indian has heard of the Tatas and the Birlas. But while the Tatas have been content to strengthen their original reputation, Kumar has created a sub-brand within the Birla image: the Aditya Birla Group with its distinctive logo. Many young people, I tell him, now think of the sun when you mention the Birlas, not recognizing that it is the logo of just one part of the whole family business.

In the process, he has become one of India's most respected businessmen. While many of the traditional bania families are seen as being too old-economy or as being creations of the license-quota-permit raj, he has led a Birla renaissance. Even people who are unaware of G.D. Birla's friendship with Mahatma Gandhi or of the Birla family's role in India's independence struggle, will look up to Kumar Birla as epitomizing the best qualities of Indian business.

Kumar does not agree. He does not believe that he is treated any differently from any other member of his family or that his Aditya Birla Group now has a reputation for integrity and excellence that is matched only by the Tatas and the Bangalore IT companies.

Why create a sub-brand then? I ask.

' It started out as an internal touch-point. I wanted to capture certain values that I wanted the group to embody: youth, dynamism, trust, tradition, modernity, growth and quality. These are the values that I strive for and I wanted some way of embodying them.'

But surely, the youth bit is his contribution? The Birlas are an old family. He is the young element in that brand image?

'Perhaps. But a brand is not about individuals. Whatever it stands for is really a tribute to the team we have created ... '

Sensing that he is about to go all-modest on me again, I ask him about his destiny. Supposing his surname had not been Birla; suppose he had not inherited this Rs 8,000 crore empire; what would Kumar Birla have done then?

'The same thing. Though perhaps without all these advantages. I would still have been an entrepreneur.'

So that's how he sees himself? Not as a captain of industry? Not as a great manager? But as a simple entrepreneur?

'Oh yes. That's what I am. I am an entrepreneur.'

And he enjoys that?

'Yes. That is my passion. That is my whole life.' And with so much passion in him, how could I have ever made the mistake of believing that he worries about being boring?

sunil bharati mittal

Chairman and MD, Bharti Group

▲

There's something slightly scary about Sunil Mittal's success. I first met him over a decade ago and he was already successful enough. Airtel had launched its mobile service in the Delhi circle. The Mittal brothers had their Beetel brand of digital telephones and Sunil had all the outward trappings of success: he'd bought his first Mercedes many years before.

But there was nothing about Sunil or about the business environment as it then existed to suggest that he would ever reach the stage he is at today. I recall a discussion programme on Doordarshan in the pre-satellite news channel days. We were talking about the telecom revolution and Sunil was one of the guests while I was the moderator. It was just after the second round of telephone licences and Airtel had done badly, winning only the Himachal Pradesh circle.

Though there were many other guests on the programme, including a former telecom secretary, the star of the show was Mahendra Nahata of Himachal Futuristic. This was when Nahata's company (HFCL, for short) had won several licences on the back of telecom minister Sukh Ram's support and most people regarded HFCL as the future of Indian telecom.

[' ... I told my people that I knew that we were not expected to win. But I would tell them, if we can win against the odds, then we make history.']

I asked Nahata the question everybody was asking: how on earth did he expect to generate the huge profits from telecom that his bids had projected? Nahata was confident, cocky even. Sunil, on the other hand, was low-key. Why, I asked, had he lost out to the likes of HFCL?

'I don't have the money,' he smiled. But when I asked whether he believed Nahata's projections were valid, he turned sombre. The telecom business was headed for a huge shake-out some years down the line, he said quietly. He did not share the optimism of many of his competitors. 'There will,' he said firmly, 'be blood on the streets.'

Everybody knows what happened in the decade that followed. The blood overflowed through the roads and avenues of our metropolises. Sukh Ram went to jail. Nahata's projections were trounced by reality. And as the bust began to take hold, Sunil and Airtel swooped down on the bleeding licencees and bought them all out.

Today, Airtel has a national network with a presence in nearly every major sector. The company is among India's largest and its market capitalization is Rs 60,000 crore. Sunil and his brothers own 32 per cent of the company and are therefore worth something like Rs 20,000 crore.

And yet, when you meet him, he is still the same low-key guy who came to the Doordarshan studio. He doesn't seem poor or unsuccessful but he doesn't act as though he is much richer than he was a decade ago. (Much richer? He was probably worth much under Rs 100 crore in those days, a far cry from today's Rs 20,000 crore.) How did he do it? How does he explain the spectacular success?

Sunil says he has no real explanation. And then comes the really scary bit: 'The only answer I can give is that there is a divine purpose. God has some plan for me. And I am merely executing his plan. I can't think of any other explanation for our success.'

When we called him the messiah of the telecom sector, we had no idea that this was what it meant.

Rise to riches

The broad outlines of Sunil Mittal's rise to riches are well known. It is a story that Sunil tells particularly well himself. Four years ago, I had him on my Star Talk programme, one of his first full-length television appearances, and he ended up being one of the show's best-ever guests because he spoke with such sincerity and intensity about how he'd made it to the big league.

For those of you who missed the story that has now been featured prominently by every business magazine in the country, it goes something like this: Sunil's father war Satpaul Mittal, a well-respected and much-liked politician from Ludhiana. The older Mittal had three sons, all of whom went into business (they are still partners in Airtel) but the star was always Sunil.

He started small, both in terms of age and vision. When he was nineteen, he began to import scrap and then moved into bicycle parts. Next came a small-scale project to manufacture stainless steel sheets. This took him out of Ludhiana and to Mumbai where he had to sell his product. He has fond memories, he says, of sitting on low stools in small cubicles in Pydhonie and Abdul Rehman Street, trying to persuade traders to buy his sheets.

The Bombay experience taught him two things. First, that he was a natural salesman. And second, that he had to get out of Ludhiana. As long as the Mittals remained a Punjab-based family, they would always be small-time. He needed to move to a big city, to be near the action, and to learn to think big.

In 1979, Sunil moved to the small MP's flat that his father had been allotted in Delhi. At a time when everybody dreamed of being an exporter, Sunil moved into imports instead. He made huge profits importing steel and zip fasteners till one day, he ran into a harassed Japanese salesman in the capital's Bengali Market.

The salesman worked for Suzuki and had been sent to India to find a dealer for the company's generators. Suzuki operated on the assumption that the Indian market would mirror the rest of the world where generators were used to power fairs, outdoor exhibitions and hot-dog stands. Sunil knew better. He realized that in a country that was always short of power, he could sell generators to households that wanted an alternative during electricity cuts.

The Suzuki salesman had to be persuaded to appoint Sunil as his dealer but once Sunil got the business, he quickly created the consumer genset market and in no time at all was the largest importer of Suzuki generators in the whole world. He says now that the experience was a turning point in his life. He learnt to do business with foreigners and moved into the branded product sector.

By the early 1980s, Sunil was a millionaire. The genset business was booming. He had a flair for trading and he'd made a fortune from property development. Inevitably, the big boys cast a covetous eye on his sector. In 1983, the Birlas and the Shrirams were given licences to manufacture gensets in India. To protect this developing industry, the government promptly banned all generator imports.

Sunil was out of business.

He scrambled to find alternative sources of income. The Suzuki company, sympathetic to his predicament, recommended that he be appointed a dealer for the new Maruti Suzuki car. Remembers Sunil, 'All the other dealers were appointed on the basis of political influence. The only single request that Suzuki made was that I should be given a dealership. Even then, they turned me down and gave it to somebody else.'

Is Sunil bitter about the failure to land the dealership?

'Not at all. In those days there was lots of money in a Maruti dealership. If they had made me a dealer, then I would have got rich and comfortable. Looking back, I think that it was God's design that I should not get too comfortable. He had other plans for me.'

Indeed, He did.

The big break

Searching for a new business opportunity, Sunil ended up in Taiwan, where he saw a push-button phone. He decided that this was the future and began to import the components for the phone, entirely illegally, as far as I can tell, and launched it in the Indian market. He chose the brand name Mitbrau.

That sounds very German, I tell him.

'Exactly, that was the idea,' he explains. 'Actually all it meant was Mittal brothers, but I wanted to make it sound like a foreign brand name because I had learnt that Indian consumers didn't like *desi* brands.'

Fortunately, the government opened up the telecom market and the Mittals were among the fifty-two businesses chosen to manufacture telephones and handsets. His business, using the brand name Beetel, did well with sales of about Rs 25 crore – a huge sum in those days – but Sunil was not satisfied. He could see beyond the nice house and the Mercedes and sensed that no matter how comfortable he was, the Mittals were still very far from the big-time.

The big break came in 1992, when the government invited bids for mobile telephony. Sunil saw the story about the bids in the *Economic Times* when he was in Goa for a New Year holiday and decided that he was going to be among the bidders. Sadly, his father died within days. Even so, as heartbroken as he was, he took six months off from the family business to put together his master plan for mobile telephony.

People forget now that when the Government of India first opened up the telecom sector, nearly every global telecom player made a beeline for India. Among these experienced multinational players, the Mittals seemed like ignorant pygmies. But Sunil was sure that he could put together a consortium with many of the foreign players and still make a valid bid.

The problem was that he didn't have much money and he certainly didn't have much in the way of reputation. What he did have, however, was his personal charisma. He has a unique ability to win people over in one-on-one encounters and if you push him, he will admit that his speciality consists of persuading people to go further than they had originally planned through the sheer force of his personality.

For instance, he pushed Vivendi into going with him after a single meeting. Later, after the deal had been signed, the company sent a team to India to check out exactly who the Mittals were. The team reported back that they were small-timers and likely to remain so. Vivendi pulled the plug days before the bid was to be submitted.

It was time for Sunil to work the phone. He called the company in Paris. 'Look,' he said, 'when you agreed to go with me, you sensed something. You saw something in me. Remember that something. Go with your instincts. Forget what your team has told you.'

Against the odds, Vivendi stuck with him.

When the bids were opened, Airtel had won all four circles. The government promptly declared that it had a new rule: one company, one circle. So, Sunil was left with one of the two Delhi licences.

In retrospect, he says, it was just as well that they started with a single circle. He had clearly underestimated the work required in setting up a mobile phone business. And Delhi, in itself, was more than he could handle.

Airtel did well enough in Delhi but when the second round of licences were awarded, the company only won Himachal Pradesh. With the multinationals still in the game, and such players as HFCL on the rise, sceptics wondered whether a family-run single circle company could survive.

This was when I shot that Doordarshan discussion with Sunil. I ask him about it and he says he remembers the programme well. His modesty was genuine, he says. 'I spent days trying to work out how we had been outbid. And try as I might I could not see how the winning bids could possibly be workable. When I told you that there would be blood in the streets, I was being realistic. I knew then that all we had to do was hang on.' Well, yes and no. The biggest challenge was still to come.

Difficult periods

In 1999, the mobile telephone industry was in bad shape. The operators could not pay the huge licence fees they had promised the government. Eventually, a new formula was worked out. The industry would migrate to a revenue-sharing model. But before this could happen, the government asked operators to clear all existing dues.

Sunil had guessed that this was coming. Airtel had talked to its bankers and gathered a substantial war-chest. When many operators could not clear their dues, Sunil swooped down and bought up their licences. At a stroke, he acquired Andhra, Karnataka, Chennai and Punjab. Later, he bought out the Modis from Kolkata. In the process, he had nearly every major city in India except for Mumbai.

That was rectified when the government announced bids for a fourth licence. Airtel won eight new circles: Gujarat, MP, Tamil Nadu, Kerala, Maharashtra, Western UP and Mumbai. In five years, Sunil had gone from being the man who had lost out to HFCL to becoming the Mobile King of India.

But, the genset experience was about to repeat itself: the Big Boys wanted their share of the market.

When the Ambanis announced that they were entering the mobile telephone sector with CDMA technology (as distinct from Sunil's GSM phones), the general view was that Airtel was in trouble. The Ambanis were big. They were smart. They had never failed at anything they had tried. And they had the Government of India wrapped up no matter which party was in power.

As though the mere entry of Reliance wasn't enough of a threat, government policies were amended to favour CDMA operators who had much lower entry costs (and were therefore to claim that CDMA was a cheaper technology) and then, BSNL announced that it would set up its own low-price network.

The general view was that the mobile telephony market would now be transformed. Till then, mobile phones had been a rich man's tool. Now, between the Ambanis and BSNL, they would undercut the expensive GSM operators and win over their customers with lower rates.

Everybody I know bought the logic and within Airtel, the mood was gloomy. Each year, the company holds a conclave of its senior managers to plan strategy. In 2002, this conclave was held at the Mughal Sheraton in Agra and it was something of a crisis session. 'We knew that we were fighting for our survival,' Sunil remembers. 'The company was polarized between two points of view. Some people said that we should go out and fight. I had an opposite view because I knew what we were up against. My strategy was to lie low and conserve our energies. Wait till the storm passes and see what the situation is like then. In the interim, we would do our best to get close to the customer.'

Because Sunil was lying low, there was intense speculation about his future course of action. It was no secret that he shared his father's fascination with politics. One view had it that he would sell out and enter politics as a very rich man. Another view was that SingTel, a major investor in Airtel, would pay off the Mittals and take effective control of the company. Almost nobody thought that he would take on the might of the Ambanis.

The bad phase lasted a year and he says now that it was one of the most difficult periods in his life. 'Because morale was so low, I went around meeting our people and giving them hope. I began to watch movies in which the underdog won, the sort of story where guerillas defeated a big army. Everywhere I went, I told my people that I knew that we were not expected to win. But, I would tell them, if we can win against the odds, then we make history.'

It was a story with a happy ending. The Reliance venture is not a failure by any standards. It has around 10-12 million subscribers against Airtel's 14 million. But it has made no dent in the business of the big GSM operators. Instead, two distinct markets have developed. The top end is dominated by Airtel. The cheap telephony market is Reliance's own. And of course, the big profits lie in the top end.

Remembers Sunil, ' In 2003, we had our conclave in Bangkok and the change in mood was so palpable that we called it a victory conclave and treated ourselves like people who had won Olympic gold medals. When you think back, it is amazing how quickly things changed in a single year.'

No politics

So, now that he has held his own against the might of the Ambanis, what will Sunil Mittal do next? He denies strenuously that he had ever intended to sell out to SingTel. He does admit that he had planned to enter politics by the time he was fifty – in 2007.

But he says that his plans have changed. He has lost his fascination for politics. He has seen other business people enter Parliament and does not believe that they have been able to make a significant difference. He has also recognized that as a member of a political party, he will be subject to party discipline and unable to say what he truly feels.

His conclusion is that he can contribute much more to society by staying out of politics and remaining the master of his own businesses. He quotes Christopher Bland, the chairman of British Telecom, who asked him one day whether he intended to join politics. Taken by surprise, Sunil blurted out the truth: he was toying with the idea. ' Do yourself a favour,' Bland told him. 'Each time you feel like joining politics, go and take a shower.'

And yet, he senses that there is much more to come in his life. He has, by his own calculation, at least another twenty years of working life left. Because he believes that so much of his success has nothing to do with him but is part of some divine plan, he is not sure what the next phase will be.

I ask him why he keeps attributing his achievements to God. In nearly every interview, divine intervention plays a starring role. For instance, when he appeared on the cover of *HT*'s supplement *Brunch*, he declared, ' When I look back at this fairy-tale story, it is clear that there has been divine intervention at every stage. It was meant to be.'

In somebody else's mouth, the words could sound arrogant or even, slightly loony – a sort of crazy suggestion that he is the chosen one – but Sunil manages to make them sound humble. My theory is that he finds his success scarier than he is willing to admit. I know of no Indian businessman who has grown as fast as he has in the face of such odds. And I think that at some level, he needs to convince himself that it was destiny rather than his own ability that ensured his success.

Certainly, when you speak to him, there is none of the boastful arrogance that characterizes many other self-made men. Instead, there is an endearing honesty. He does not need to admit, for instance, that the Mitbrau imports may well have been illegal. Nor does he need to reveal quite how despondent he got during his low phases. Even when he discusses his successes, he is matter of fact about his silver-tongued ability to persuade people to bet on him even when his credentials do not justify the size of the bet.

I tell him that one of the joys of interviewing businessmen for this Leadership Series lies in discovering people whom nobody would have bothered with even fifteen years ago: Nandan Nilekani, Rajiv Chandrasekhar, Subhash Chandra, Uday Kotak, Azim Premji, and of course, Sunil Mittal himself.

'That's the great thing about today's India,' he says. 'When people come and interview me, I always tell them to focus on the fact that we were able to create one of the world's top mobile telephone companies in the space of a decade without having to cheat anybody and break any laws. It can be done. And I would encourage more people to try and do it.'

With or without divine intervention, of course.

fighting a good fight

rajeev chandrasekhar
Former Chairman & CEO, BPL Mobile

▲

ere's the funny thing about Rajeev Chandrasekhar. Actually, here is a whole list of funny things. Funny thing one: more people have heard of Chandrasekhar now than had ever heard of him when he was actually running his business. Now that he has sold BPL Mobile to the Ruias of Essar (and therefore, eventually, to Hutch), he is on every TV channel and in every business paper. Selling a company for a figure north of $ 1.1 billion will do that for you every time.

Funny thing number two: everyone sees his picture in the papers and assumes that he is some rich kid, part of the BPL dynasty, who has struck some big deal that has made the family rich. Actually, this is not quite true.

And funny thing number three: though his is a genuine new economy success story on par with Infosys, Wipro and all the others, Rajeev – like all the telecom whizkids – never gets the credit that is his due.

From Intel to India
The thing to remember about Chandrasekhar, no matter how many times you see him on CNBC holding forth about

> 'By 2001, BPL Mobile had become India's largest operator without my having to go to a single politician or pay a single bribe.'

telecom policy, is that he is not really from the world of business.

Like the Nandan Nilekanis before him (he is a decade younger than Nandan and thus part of the next generation of tech whizkids), Chandrasekhar has not a drop of entrepreneurial blood in his veins. His background is solidly professional: his father was an air force officer. The young Rajeev grew up in a series of air force stations, in Jorhat, Ladakh and Delhi Cantt. He had no interest in business and never believed that he would run a company.

He claims to have been solidly average in academic terms but got into Manipal to do an under-graduate degree in engineering. Even so, his memories of college are not the usual geek stories that the IIT types who dominate the IT industry are fond of retelling. His strongest memory is of being part of a gang of bikers called the Junk Sangh (ironic, in the light of the friends he made later in life, but don't even ask) who would drive down to Bangalore for concerts by the few rock stars who came to India in the 1980s: Wishbone Ash, Uriah Heep, and the other washed-up Brit bands who had hit the Third World trail.

In 1984, he went to the Illinois Institute in Chicago for a post-graduate degree and his chief memory of August 1984 is of being mugged on his first day in the US. But he can't have been as moderately intelligent as he now claims to have been. He finished his degree in nine months and gained a mentor to beat all mentors, Vinod Dham, then not quite the legend he was later to become at Intel.

Chandrasekhar had many offers when he finished his degree, but he chose Intel over Microsoft because of Dham's influence. It was a wise decision. He got to Silicon Valley as the boom was just beginning and the tech whizkids were still entrepreneurs and hadn't yet bought their yachts and Merlot vineyards.

He has records, he says, of meetings he attended where Bill Gates was another participant and he remembers discussing things with Larry Ellison in the Intel café. Chandrasekhar was one of Intel's fastest rising stars and became one of only three engineers who were CPU architects, working on the next generation of chips. Every Intel 486 processor ever manufactured, contains his initials, along with those of the thirty other engineers who worked on the project.

Why then, did he come back from Silicon Valley?

At the end of the 1980s, he met Anju, who was doing an MBA in Boston and the two decided to get married. Anju was the daughter of the founder of BPL and after what he calls the usual round of Malayali investigations – 'making sure I didn't have an American mistress on the side' – her parents were pleased to consent to the match. Rajeev says that they never minded that his own family was solidly middle class; the Nambiars of BPL, like all good Malayalis, valued education over wealth.

He took a year of absence from Intel after getting married and came back to India. Through one of those coincidences that end up changing lives, his father introduced him to Rajesh Pilot, whom he had taught to fly during Rajesh's air force days. Rajesh took him to meet Rajiv Gandhi – who was then in Opposition – and asked him the obvious question: why not come back to India and help prepare the country for the electronic revolution of the twenty-first century?

Chandrasekhar was intrigued. He was having a great time in Silicon Valley. His career was zooming and he was listening to B.B. King and Robert Cray – live. But somewhere in his heart, he knew that there was a life beyond the blues.

A life in Bangalore, perhaps.

Reality check

In 1991, when Rajeev Chandrasekhar first got into business in India, he rejected the software option in favour of something that seemed even more novel. In the early 1990s, mobile telephony was not big in the US though there was a boom in Europe. But Chandrasekhar found good partners in France Telecom and Craig McCaw; used his father-in-law's brand name; and bid for the first round of cellular licences.

In 1994, when the licences finally came through, after endless rounds of litigation, he moved to Mumbai from Bangalore, hired a 1,000 square foot office in Arcadia at Nariman Point, borrowed Rs 100 crore from IDBI, staffed his operation with youngsters and ex-military men and tried to drag India into the cellular age.

Almost from the word go, things went according to plan. The bidding process was completely transparent. Nobody asked him for a bribe at IDBI. And Rajeev began to believe that he would repeat the experience of the software successes and create an honest, world-class business for the new India.

In 1996, when Sukh Ram, then telecom minister, announced another round of bidding, Rajeev was not perturbed. In the last five years he had never needed to meet a minister so when the bureaucrats told him to call on Sukh Ram, he was not only surprised but also quite excited – 'it seemed like a real big deal to have a one-on-one with a minister,' he remembers.

Sukh Ram went round and round in circles and then invited him for a second meeting. After this encounter when Chandrasekhar still failed to see the point, he finally asked in desperation, ' Isn't there any older person in your house whom I can talk to?' But there wasn't. Because this was a young business. And though Sukh Ram did his little fiddles to benefit Himachal Futuristic, denying BPL Mobile some of the circles it had bid for, Chandrasekhar was able to say that he had managed to become the biggest operator in the mobile telephony business without paying a single significant bribe.

Till then, he says, with just a trace of irony, his experience paralleled that of his software billionaire Bangalore buddies.

The Idea that went wrong

By 2001, BPL Mobile was the largest cellular operator in India. And Chandrasekhar had become the poster boy of the telecom revolution – the Intel engineer who came back to India to prepare us for the twenty-first century.

Then, things began to go wrong. He made one mistake. And he suffered one assault from which he never quite recovered.

The mistake was to get involved with what was then known as the Batata Conglomerate. Kumar Mangalam Birla, Ratan Tata and AT&T decided to come together to create a new company that would be professionally managed and would have no controlling shareholder. Chandrasekhar decided to merge BPL Mobile into the big Batata, recognizing that his company, by virtue of its size, would be the single largest shareholder in the new entity.

An MOU was signed in 2001 and Chandrasekhar sat back. He did not invest further in the business, did not prevent subscribers from migrating and waited for the new conglomerate to take shape.

And take shape it did. Except that BPL Mobile was not part of the entity that eventually became Idea. In 2002, the MOU expired and Idea said that it had no interest in renewing it.

Despite having lost market share, Chandrasekhar and BPL were on their own.

What went wrong? Market gossip has it that the Tatas were content with the deal but that the Birlas were not comfortable with the idea of playing junior partner to Rajeev Chandrasekhar.

So, was he diddled by Kumar Mangalam Birla?

Rajeev Chandrasekhar looks disturbed. 'I'm not going to point fingers at anybody. Let's just say the deal didn't work out,' he snaps shortly.

Battle won, war lost

Though nobody saw this at the time, the Batata fiasco marked the end of BPL's national ambitions. Chandrasekhar had been willing to sit back when rivals were grabbing market share. And now, that smugness came back to haunt him as competitors like Airtel raced ahead of BPL in the national marketplace.

One reason why the enormity of the error remained hidden was because Chandrasekhar was back in the news for much of this period as the head of the cellular operators association, fighting a very public battle for reform of the licensing policy.

Even as he explained why the industry was doomed unless the arrangement was shifted to profit-sharing, few people noticed that BPL had missed out completely on the bidding for the fourth licences. Had there been no Idea merger on the cards, BPL would certainly have bid for Delhi. But the entire expansion passed Chandrasekhar by and as new giants emerged, BPL lost its pre-eminent position in the Indian cellular market.

But even as he was losing market share, Chandrasekhar won the bigger battle for the cellular industry. The government agreed to migrate to a profit-sharing arrangement and the operators, many of whom were hugely in debt, found their fortunes swinging skywards.

His success in that battle probably made him less prepared to face the WLL/CDMA onslaught.

When the cellular licences had been issued, the operators had been assured that nobody else would be allowed to offer cellular services. But the Vajpayee government turned this rule on its head by declaring that private operators who were offering fixed line services could also offer cellular operations, provided they used CDMA or WLL technology rather than the GSM technology favoured by the existing operators.

This move was sought to be justified on socialistic grounds. CDMA was a new technology, we were told. It was much cheaper than GSM. The new CDMA phones would be *janta* mobiles, available to the common man for a song compared to the expensive, rich man's GSM phones.

When the GSM operators objected, they were portrayed as disgruntled oligopolists fighting to prevent Indian consumers from enjoying the benefits of cheaper, newer technology. Everyone could have a mobile now, the government said, if only the GSM operators would allow this new cheap technology to reach the masses.

These arguments still anger Chandrasekhar. 'First of all,' he says, 'we didn't choose GSM. The government chose it for us. Secondly, both technologies are contemporary. CDMA is not the latest technology. Thirdly, it is not cheaper than GSM. CDMA phones are actually more expensive than GSM phones. Fourthly, the only reason it would be cheaper in India was because the CDMA operators were not being charged the high start-up costs that GSM operators had been subjected to. And finally, there was a moral issue: the GSM operators were paying for licences to operate cellular services on the understanding that the market would be restricted to a certain number of players. If we had known that the market would be opened up for free to new CDMA players, we might never have got into the business.'

These are good arguments, but though the GSM operators, headed by Chandrasekhar, made their case forcefully, they never had the impact they had hoped for. All talk of a telecom scam fell flat – until recently, when one by-product of the battle between the Ambanis was the revelation that the BJP government was clearly on the take – and there was little public pressure to amend the policy.

Finally, the GSM operators had their day in court. The Supreme Court ruled that the government policy had been malafide and illegal and ordered the construction of a more level playing field.

It was good news for the GSM industry. But it was already too late for BPL Mobile.

A Pit-stop in the pits

While Chandrasekhar was fighting these public battles, his company was going down the drain. It never recovered from the year he took off during the failed Batata merger and not only did his rivals race past him, but BPL Mobile's financial problems multiplied.

He was in default to lenders, creditors lined up outside his door, and Motorola filed a winding-up petition arguing that the company was in no position to pay its debts.

It was the lowest period of Chandrasekhar's life and he freely admits now that he spent several months wallowing in self-pity. ' I kept asking myself,' he remembers, 'how could have things changed so quickly. Till 2001, my success story was the same as any of the software guys. But by 2003, creditors were ready to close my company down.'

His conclusion: ' The software industry doesn't need to go to politicians. Most of its customers are abroad. We were entirely dependent on government and on regulators who were sometimes biased or corrupt. Till 2001, the big boys of Indian industry hadn't worried about the cellular industry. But when they did, we realized, to our cost, how completely outclassed we were. They either diddled us or swung government policy against us. I had no idea how bad or how damaging corporate sabotage could be.'

He pauses. ' The thing I've learnt about India,' he says, 'is that if one of the big boys wants to destroy you and knows how to manipulate the government, then there is nothing you can do.'

Life begins at forty

But, of course, there was something he could do. Chandrasekhar threw himself back into the business, determined to pull BPL Mobile out of the hole it had dug itself into. In 2002-03, the company had seen virtually no growth.

In 2003-04, growth had been 14 per cent. But with Chandrasekhar determined to do better, the business grew by an astonishing 58 per cent in 2004-05.

Against the odds, he had pulled the company back from the brink. Admittedly, he was no longer the poster boy of mobile telephony – that title now belonged to Sunil Mittal of Airtel – but he wasn't a failure either. He had a successful business that was growing at a healthy rate.

Just when it seemed his problems were over, a new complication arose. His father-in-law decided to fight him in the courts. The Chandrasekhar position, as described by his lawyers, was that BPL Mobile was always his own business. He paid a licence fee to his in-laws for the BPL brand but that was all. He ran the business himself, found his own financing, and was treated as a separate entity by markets and bankers. The problem was that the mother brand was no longer doing well and that BPL Mobile now had lots of money. It was, says Chandrasekhar, a difficult time because of the family complications. He refused to say a word against his father-in-law, asked Anju not to take sides and continued to send his children to meet their grandparents. ' I decided that I would treat it as a business problem, not as a family dispute,' he recalls.

That approach worked and in July 2005 the dispute was settled amicably. Chandrasekhar decided to give up the BPL brand and as he considered creating a new branding, he mandated Morgan Stanley to find a 40 per cent equity partner. But, the more he thought about it, the more sense it made to just sell out and take the money. When a good offer from Essar came along in June 2005, he decided to end one chapter of his life.

He is prohibited from saying how much the deal valued BPL Mobile at. He won't even comment on market speculation that it was around $ 1.2 billion. He will admit, however, that he is now a very rich man, though his preferred phrasing is, 'let's just say that I am now very comfortably off.'

He has many plans: he wants to start a venture capital fund; he has a passion for publishing; a foundation is in the works; he will spend more time on the hotel he owns in Kovalam; and, of course, he is looking at new investments in the technology sector.

Given how much he has gone through in the last decade, it is sometimes easy to forget how young he is: just forty. In many ways, he still has his life in front of him.

It's been a long, strange ride, I tell him. Has his story demonstrated that middle-class techies may do well with foreign customers but are screwed over much too easily by the experienced bania businesses?

He is not sure, he says. ' My career had two phases. If you look at what happened to me after 2001, I would say you were right. But let's not forget that I bid for my licences in 1991. And by 2001,

BPL Mobile had become India's largest operator without my having to go to a single politician or pay a single bribe.'

The final, inevitable question: didn't the telecom industry commit an error by getting the stubborn and self-righteous Rajeev to fight its battle? There are other telecom entrepreneurs who are much more realistic and could have cut the right kind of deal with the government.

At first, he bristles at the suggestion. 'I don't think the ends justify the means,' he says angrily. But then, he makes a valid point: 'You know who we were up against. If we had offered a bribe of x, they would have offered a bribe of 4x. We couldn't have bought our way out of this one. We had no choice but to fight.'

Rajeev Chandrasekhar's fighting days are, thank God!, finally over. He has lost seventeen kilos in four months, went easy on the food and the vodka, found more time for his Lamborghini and flew to London to catch the Cream reunion concert. He has no regrets, he says. But yes, he is relieved.

Oh yes, he is very relieved.

there's more to life

azim premji

Chairman & MD, Wipro Limited

▲

I t is not easy to interview Azim Premji. The process begins with
the Wipro PR department saying it will consider the request.
Then, there is a demand for a questionnaire. What would I like
to know?

It doesn't work that way, I respond. The point of these
profiles is that I try and go beyond the statistics and find the
individual at the core of the business.

Well, okay, Wipro's PR department e-mails back. I can meet
Premji but he still wants the questions beforehand because 'Azim
is much better on e-mail.'

I rack my brains for questions. Eventually, I send off all the
obvious ones. How does it feel to be India's richest man at the
turn of the century? Why do all his number twos seem to leave?
Does he think of himself as a Gujarati?

The Wipro PR people e-mail back: is that all? We thought you
were going to do a long piece on Premji. But you've sent only six
questions.

I explain again that I'm not really interested in Wipro's
business plan. The idea is to try and understand the man himself.

They remain unconvinced but we agree on a deal. Premji will
respond to my questions on e-mail and then, we can meet for

[
'I was brought up to believe that values
are more important than money.'
]

lunch at Wipro's Bangalore campus. The lunch will be a largely social occasion, a chance to get to meet the man, and, perhaps, ask any supplementary questions not covered in the original questionnaire.

And so, I find myself in Bangalore waiting for one of Premji's aides to pick me up from my hotel and take me to lunch with the man himself. There has been no response to my questionnaire, so I'm not quite sure how I will be able to ask follow-up questions, given that I don't have answers to the first lot.

Perhaps the answers will come later, I decide. Let's just enjoy the lunch. It's values, not money. Wipro has many offices in Bangalore. I've seen one, in Electronics City, near the Infosys campus. But the space where Premji works is very different from the chrome and glass structures of Electronic City. It is soft, green and could well have been designed as the headquarters of a back-to-nature NGO.

Adjacent to the cafeteria is a small private dining room and it is here that we are to eat lunch. Seconds after I enter the room, Premji appears. He looks rather as he does in his photographs, a quiet, intense man whose distinguishing characteristic is his thick white hair. He is wearing a white shirt with a Wipro logo on his left pocket and though we are in his own dining room, he seems shy and strangely awkward.

I have some idea of what the food is going to be like. The PR department had called ahead to ask if I was a vegetarian. When I said that I ate everything, they asked if Chinese food would be okay.

So when the waiters bring bowls of sweet corn soup, I am not particularly surprised. Premji makes some attempt at small talk. Inevitably, the conversation turns to the collapsing infrastructure of Bangalore. I tell him how appalled I am by the deterioration in the quality of life in what used to be one of India's nicest cities.

Premji is as appalled. 'But I've decided not to talk too much about it after the last time,' he says. Some years ago he had criticized the government for its neglect of Bangalore and evoked angry responses from politicians.

'It used to be so different,' he recalls. 'I remember when we were young, we used to sometimes come here on holiday and it was like a hill station. A friend of my father had a seven-acre property on MG Road and the whole place was so green. Even in the 1980s, it was still a very nice place to live.'

Since he has brought up the subject of his childhood, I decide that we might as well begin the interview – to the extent that this lunch can be called an interview – with his background.

Though Infosys and Wipro are the two great IT companies, the backgrounds of their promoters could not be more different. Infosys is the creation of engineers from lower-middle-class backgrounds. Wipro has its origins in the Premji family's edible oil business (the company's original name was Western Indian Vegetable Products Ltd.) and though Azim studied electrical engineering at Stanford, he is not a techie in the sense that NarayanMurthy and Nandan Nilekani are. Instead, he is a businessman who is still as proud of the other things that Wipro does (apart from IT), including its Consumer Care business that produces the popular Santoor soap. Whereas most IT success stories represent a sort of Revenge of the Nerds formula, Wipro's success is about timely diversification in a traditional business.

How affluent was Premji's family? I ask. Did he feel rich when he was growing up?

'Well, I knew we were comfortable,' he says. 'But there was no sense in which I was conscious of belonging to a rich family.'

Did his family have many cars?

He pauses. 'We had two cars,' he says, conscious that this was unusual in an era when most middle-class Indian families could not afford a single car. 'But they were Indian cars, not imported.'

His family had enough money to send him to America for further studies in the 1960s, I say. That suggests a certain level of affluence. 'Yes, but I remember that I was allowed to come back to India only once a year. And it was a really big thing for me. I used to look forward to it.'

And did he fly economy class?

'Oh, always. Even my children travel economy class.'

And why is that?

'Values, I was brought up to believe that values are more important than money.'

Animal in a zoo

By this time, the soup bowls have been removed and we are on to the noodles.

Premji eats without taking any real interest in the food, but he is noticeably more relaxed now than he was when the soup was being served.

It is, I decide, a good time to ask him the question that everyone wants to know the answer to.

How does it feel to be India's richest man with a fortune that is estimated at over $10 billion?

'Like an animal in a zoo,' he says shortly. 'I hate it when people only talk about my wealth. For many years, all the articles would focus only on how much money I had. As though there was nothing else in my life.'

They still do, I tell him.

'Less and less. I'm very grateful that L.N. Mittal is so much richer than me,' he laughs. 'All the articles about billionaires now are about Mittal and, fortunately, I am spared. I read last week that even Mukesh Ambani will soon be ahead of me. That is a great relief because I hate answering questions about my wealth.'

Was there a time when he suddenly felt, 'Oh my God! I am now the richest man in India?'

'No, it happened gradually, so I suppose I was less aware of it till the press made me aware of it every day. There was one big jump which I noticed but after that it was gradual.'

He is so rich, I say, because he owns three-fourths of Wipro. Hasn't there even been the temptation to sell part of his stock (as say, the promoters of Infosys have done) to unlock some of the money?

'What would I do with the money? You can't spend so much cash. I would have to invest it in something. And if I am going to invest it, then why not keep it invested in Wipro?'

But does he feel rich?

'Even when I was young, my family never believed in spending much money or in conspicuous consumption. If we went for a holiday, it would be to Mahabaleshwar or some place like that. We wouldn't go abroad. I still have that same attitude to money.'

A little help from religion

Most rich people usually say the same things: that the money doesn't matter; that one can only spend so much in a lifetime etc. (Unless, of course, you are interviewing Vijay Mallya who says none of these things.) But the importance of Premji's wealth is that it is a symbol.

For years and years, critics of Indian secularism would show us lists of the hundred largest companies in the country and point out that there was not one Muslim-owned unit among them. Of course, there were rich Muslims. In such fields as edible oils, Gujarati Muslims (such as Premji's family) had a traditional presence. But there was a kind of glass ceiling that no Muslim could ever hope to break.

Now, at a stroke, Premji has turned the conventional wisdom on its head. Not only is he very rich, he is also the richest man in India. Does he recognize the enormity of this achievement?

Premji is clearly uncomfortable with questions that focus on his religion. Though he answers in a quiet voice, I can sense the irritation – and slight defensiveness – in his tone.

'I have never thought of myself as a Muslim. Or a Gujarati. Or as anything other than a citizen of India,' he says.

So he doesn't see his success as proof of the strength of Indian secularism.

'You don't need to look at me if you want proof of Indian secularism,' he says. 'Just look at the people in this country who are on top. Our president is a Muslim. The prime minister is a Sikh. The Congress president was born a Roman Catholic. The leader of the opposition is a Hindu. Can you think of one other country where such a situation exists?'

Is he ducking my question?

'No, I can honestly tell you that the way I was brought up, I never thought of people as Hindus, Muslims, Sikhs or whatever. For example, at school, there were boys with Hindu names and Muslim names. But even though, in retrospect, it was obvious that some of us were Hindus and Muslims, I simply never made the connection at the time. We were just boys together. That's how I grew up, thinking of all of us as Indians.'

Has he ever felt any discrimination or sensed that he is a Muslim in a Hindu-majority country?

'No, never. Not once. In fact, these days, it is even turning out to be a positive factor,' he laughs.

Which takes us, inevitably, to Gujarat. Narendra Modi's PR machine has been trumpeting that Wipro will make huge investments in Gujarat.

'It suits them to play that up,' Premji smiles, 'only because I am a Muslim.'

But isn't it true that after the Gujarat riots, Premji had been very critical of Modi's government?

'I was shocked. I was horrified,' he says. 'I went to Ahmedabad afterwards and there was still a lot of communal tension. I'm not sure that the press accurately reported the extent of the violence. My feeling is that things were even worse than the press said they were.'

Was he reacting as a Muslim?

'Not at all. I was reacting as a citizen of India, as a human being. Any Indian – anybody, for that matter – would have been shocked by the devastation and the loss of human life. You don't have to be a Muslim to feel that way.'

And now? Has he made up with Modi?

'We are doing business in Gujarat just as we do business in other important markets. It has got nothing to do with Modi or with politics. But of course, it suits them to play it up.'

'So, you see,' he smiles, a little sardonically, 'being a Muslim can actually get you more recognition.'

The many-layered Premji

The waiters clear away the noodles and the chicken and bring us bowls of fruit. Premji sends one back, asking only for a little ice cream.

He seems relaxed enough for me to ask him why he comes across as so shy.

'Shy? If you think I am shy now,' he responds, 'you should have seen what I was like ten years ago. I am much less shy now.'

Not only does he comes across as shy, I say, he also comes across as extremely cautious.

'Yes, I am very cautious,' he concedes. 'I am not a very confident person. I take a lot of time to make key decisions. I like doing my homework before I take any decision.'

Was this why he hired Vivek Paul to be his CEO? Because Paul's publicity-loving nature made him a perfect foil for Premji's reticence?

'No,' he says, he never thought about Paul that way. 'I hired Vivek because Ashok (Soota) had left and we needed somebody to replace him. I thought of taking over myself but I did not have the confidence to do so. I have the confidence now and Wipro's second line has also developed to the extent that I can leave more things to them. But at that stage, we needed somebody to replace Ashok.'

Why Vivek Paul?

'Because he had a global outlook and the company was at the stage where we needed somebody with that approach.'

Would it be fair to say that Premji is not an easy man to work with?

'Why do you say that?' he counters.

Because, I tell him, he seems like a difficult sort of guy to understand. For a start, there is the famous shyness that makes it impossible to read him. And then, there's the intellectual subtlety of his brain. Throughout this lunch, he has struck me as a very complex man who operates on several levels simultaneously. He understands the nuances of each situation and almost everything he says is so well thought-out that it is impossible to refute. In some ways, I suggest, his brain is like an onion – each time you peel off a layer, there is another layer under it.

'I think of myself as being a straightforward person,' he says.

I don't dispute that, I tell him. Moreover, when you get past that initial shyness, there is genuine warmth that emanates from him. But he's still one hell of a complex guy.

Premji turns to the aide who has picked me up from my hotel and brought me to Wipro. 'Ask him,' he tells me. 'He works closely with me. What does he think?'

The aide tells me I have missed out on Premji's instincts. For all this talk of intellectual subtlety, many of Premji's decisions are purely instinctive.

Perhaps, I respond. But, I ask the aide, since you work so closely with him, have you ever seen him lose his temper?

He thinks for a moment. 'No,' he says, 'never.'

And is that normal? Surely everybody loses his shirt once in a while, especially a man who leads by instinct.

Premji takes the point. 'No,' he accepts. 'I'm very careful not to lose my temper when I am in office. But home is a different story. You should ask my family.'

So he does lose his temper when he is at home?

'Oh yes!'

Doesn't that suggest that he's rather more tightly controlled in office than he seems willing to admit?

Azim Premji smiles.

The battle

The broad outlines of Premji's career are well known. He took over the family business when his father died of a heart attack. He moved from vegetable oil to hydraulic cylinders and, in 1980, worked out that the exit of IBM from India had created a gap and moved into Information Technology. A series of joint ventures with GE, British Telecom and Acer helped Wipro gain entry into fresh ventures.

But, unlike Infosys, which too tried to fill the post-IBM gap, Premji also developed other businesses, including consumer products and call centres. Unlike the engineers who dominate the IT business, he is essentially an entrepreneur who takes his soap business as seriously as he regards his IT division.

What, I ask him, makes him succeed in so many different areas?

The answer seems to be that firstly, he is very hands-on. 'I do not believe you can conceive of things and then not see their execution,' he says, adding, ' even when Vivek was here, I was very hands-on.'

Secondly, he empowers people. 'I like to create businessmen,' he says. 'I encourage people to run divisions as though it is their own business. This is good because it motivates them, but bad because when it is time to move them to another division, they are reluctant to go because they have got so emotionally involved with their divisions.'

And finally, he says, he is 'cautiously paranoid'. He always recognizes, he asserts, that competitors usually do better than you give them credit for. Which, of course, leads to the obvious question: is the rivalry with Infosys genuine or is it just media hype?

'Oh, it's genuine,' he says candidly. ' At present they are growing faster than us. But let's wait and watch.'

Lessons in PR

By the time lunch is over, Premji is ready to discuss anything. Sadly, my time is up and he has other appointments.

I want to ask him more about his work in the area of education. He spends crores of his money on rural education because he believes that education is the only real solution to India's problems. But that will have to wait for another occasion.

I go back to Mumbai and wait for Wipro's PR department to respond to the written questionnaire: Azim is so much better on e-mail – remember?

By Saturday afternoon, with the deadline looming and the questions still unanswered, I decide not to wait any longer. I doubt very much if prepared answers will reveal much more of this very private, essentially cautious man.

But I would like to meet him again. You only really get to the core of the onion when you have finished peeling off the layers.

subhash chandra

Chairman, Zee Telefilms & Essel Group

▲

hy, I ask Subhash Chandra, does he maintain that distinctive lock of white hair on the front of his head? Is it a fashion statement? Does it remind him of Indira Gandhi under whose benevolence he made many crores transacting Russian rice deals?

Subhash Chandra laughs. 'Nothing like that,' he says. 'At first, it was natural, but now I have decided I like the look.'

The origin of the white tuft dates back, apparently, to Chandra's struggling days. He was about to lease a factory when his partner backed out at the last moment. 'Such was the tension and stress that this part of my hair turned white overnight. And it remained white,' he recalls.

And now? I mean, he clearly dyes his hair black, so why is that single lock exempted from the treatment?

Chandra is not offended by what many businessmen might consider a rude question. 'When I went to get my hair dyed, one day my barber told me that it might look better to keep this white. After all, that was how it had been even when the rest of my hair was black. So, I thought about it and I decided that he was probably right.'

[
'I am an enterpreneuer. I know that
I can create something from nothing.'
]

The episode should tell us three things about Chandra. One, that he enjoys his style statements. Two, that he is secure enough to discuss dyeing his hair. And three, that he hasn't had it easy. There have been very tough times and moments of incredible stress.

Feeding the army to make a living

We know Subhash Chandra as the multi-millionaire father of the Indian commercial TV revolution. His Zee TV taught Indians what televized entertainment was all about. All the other commercial Hindi channels that followed have, in one way or another, been influenced by the legacy of Zee.

We know also that he is now astonishingly rich and well connected. Ask about his net worth and first he will duck the question, saying things like, 'After the first crore, you stop counting.' But when you push, he will admit that his family has a total worth of 'around Rs 5,000 crore'. Nor will he talk about the contacts that allowed him to wage a successful battle against the global might of Rupert Murdoch. But once again, when you press, he will agree to discuss the battle even if it is only in general terms.

What we don't realize is quite how small he was when he started out. His family are Marwaris who settled in the old undivided Punjab four generations ago. They entered the grain trade and by 1966, ran one dal mill and two cotton gins.

This was small time but still it wasn't bad going. Until 1967, that is. His father lost heavily in cotton trading and the business' entire net worth was wiped out. Plus, there were debts to suppliers and moneylenders.

At the time, Chandra was seventeen and in his first year at engineering college. His father pulled him out of university and told him that he had to find some way of helping the family business.

This was easier said than done. They were bankrupt, in debt and Subhash's uncles were not sure that a seventeen-year-old had the answers to their problems.

As he remembers now, 'We had no capital to run any business, so I struggled to find something that we could do without putting in our money. Fortunately, I met the district manager of the Food Corporation of India who took a liking to me and agreed to do some business with us.'

The army was a big buyer of grains, pulses and dry fruit. But it had extraordinarily high standards and the Food Corporation was unable to meet those levels. Chandra suggested that his family could upgrade the product (polishing rice, cleaning almonds, etc.) so that it met their standards. The corporation agreed and the family was back in business because he had found a way to add value without putting in any money.

'Even then,' he says, 'we were not rich. We were still paying off debts and four families lived off the business.'

Then, in 1973-74, India had a bumper crop and the Food Corporation ran out of warehouses to store the grain. One solution was to make polythene tents to cover the mounds of wheat. Sensing an opportunity, Chandra entered this business, buying polythene sheets and then cutting them into tents. When this proved successful, he moved into making packaging material for agricultural pesticides.

In 1978, he leased an old plant in Delhi to manufacture fumigation sheets for chemicals and believed he had made the shift from agriculture to industry. In fact, he lost money on the plant. Undeterred, he imported a new technology and began making plastic tubes which he believed (correctly, as it turned out) would replace metal tubes as toothpaste containers. But even this experiment took time to take off and in the process the packaging business kept losing money.

But by 1981, these failures had ceased to worry Chandra. He had found a new way to make big money. And it had to do with grain.

Grain gain again, but with Russians

This is the bit where most profiles of Subhash Chandra suddenly begin to take on an uncertain air. We know that by 1985, he was very rich. We know also that it had to do with Russians and the Congress. But we don't quite know exactly how he made his money.

Oddly enough, Chandra has no hesitation in talking about this phase. The way it worked, he says, was this: each year the Russians would import enormous quantities of rice from India. The deal was always routed through the government, which would indicate a rice trader of its choice.

In 1981, Indira Gandhi's government told the Russians that they were to deal with Subhash Chandra. He made crores in profit on the first transaction and though he does not say so, it seems probable that some of those crores were shared with the Congress. At any rate, Mrs Gandhi was so pleased with Chandra's performance that he got the Russian rice deal every single year during her second term in office.

When Rajiv Gandhi took over, Chandra did the deal the first year and then, at the government's request, took on a 50 per cent partner in the second year. By the third year, the Congress had its own bagmen in place and he bowed out.

Is it all right to ask how much money he made on these deals, I wonder, a little tentatively. Some of it may have gone into Swiss bank accounts and I wouldn't want to embarrass him.

'No, not at all,' says Chandra. 'We took all our profits legally. They are there in our books. Many years later, when they launched income tax and FERA investigations against me, nobody was able to find anything illegal in those transactions.'

So, how much did he really make on the Russian rice deals?

'A lot of money. Lots of money. About Rs 70-80 crore, which was worth even more in those days than it is today.'

After all those years at industrial diversification, Chandra was a millionaire. And the profits had not come from industry or packaging.

They had come from the business that was in his blood: grain trading.

A Marwari ritual

What do you do when you have Rs 80 crore in cash? Either you put it into your business or you look for new investments.

Chandra did both. But first, he made his brothers go through a traditional Marwari ritual called '*pani mein namak daalna*' or literally putting salt in water. It is, he says, a sacred vow within the Marwari trading community. Once you agree to do something during this ritual, you can never back out.

The vow was: the family would be completely legit from now on. There would be no businesses that were at all underhand. Instead, they would try and do everything by the book.

As part of this endeavour, they opened the Essel Packaging plant and made huge investments in property including 800 acres in Gurgaon – Subhash had the foresight to see that as Delhi expanded, this would be a growth area.

'I think the decisions we made during that period have served us well,' he says. 'Essel Packaging now has twelve plants in eight countries. We are developing Essel Towers in Gurgaon. The land we bought in Mumbai shot up in value and we built Essel World on part of it. But the best thing we did was the *pani mein namak daalna*. So many governments have tried to investigate me but they have never found anything because I have nothing to hide.'

It was one of these decisions that led to the creation of Zee TV. Chandra built Essel World as a sort of Indian Disneyland in 1989-90 and was devastated when it failed to get the footfalls he had predicted. Consumer research led him to the conclusion that while people wanted to be entertained, they were not willing to drive two hours for this entertainment.

'The obvious thing from a business point of view was to take entertainment to people if people were not going to come to your entertainment,' he remembers. 'In those days, video was very big. So, I planned to equip a fleet of video vans that would tour the countryside charging people money to watch the videos.'

In retrospect, it doesn't seem like such a great idea, but at least it got Chandra focused on video and TV. The second idea was to run a terrestrial television station just outside the Indian border (in Nepal, perhaps) and to beam programming into the country. This too was abandoned when he realized the limitation of a terrestrial beam: it wouldn't reach any major Indian city.

Then, in 1991, watching CNN during the Gulf War, it finally came to him: why not use this new satellite technology to beam programming to India?

A STAR on the horizon

How does a wealthy Indian who has made his money in the grain trade and whose industrial experience consists of manufacturing toothpaste tubes enter the international television business?

Chandra had no idea. But he intended to find out.

He heard about Asiasat and chased the chief executive, finally locating him in the Christmas of 1991 when the man was on holiday in Canada. The Asiasat boss told Chandra that all his transponders had been leased to a new company called Satellite Television Asian Region, or STAR for short. If he wanted to run his own TV station, he needed to call STAR.

Repeated approaches to STAR headquarters in Hong Kong rarely moved higher than the level of junior executives. Eventually, because of Chandra's sheer persistence, they agreed to fix a meeting with Richard Li, son of Li Ka Shing, the owner of STAR. It was not a pleasant experience.

'We were all sitting in a room, waiting for a long time,' remembers Chandra, 'when Richard Li walked in. His executives told him that we were interested in an Indian channel. "India!" said Richard. "There is no money in India. I have no interest in India." Naturally, I was flabbergasted but kept my patience.'

The younger Li then asked Chandra, 'How much will you pay for this transponder? I don't want to do a joint venture with you so you can take the transponder on your own.'

Chandra said that a price of $1.2 million had been agreed with STAR executives.

'Not enough,' said Richard Li.

'I don't know what came over me,' recalls Chandra, 'but I got up and told him that I would take it for 5 million dollars. There was just one catch. The deal was only valid for twenty-four hours.'

If we were dealing with fiction, then Li would have said yes on the spot and Chandra would have got his transponder. But real life is never like that.

Richard Li refused to take Chandra seriously and left the room.

Enter Rupert Murdoch

By then, STAR had hired a merchant banker to advise it on potential Indian partners. The banker was scornful of Chandra who had no media credentials and sent STAR to talk to major Indian newspaper groups. But nobody was willing to pay as much as Chandra. On 21 May 1992, Richard Li finally came to India, was taken to see the Essel packaging factory, was made aware that Essel supplied to Levers', Procter & Gamble and other international companies, and finally overcame his reservations about Chandra.

And Zee TV was born.

Chandra's original business plan hoped to tap into the Rs 90 crore advertising market for video. This was not big money by any standards, so he focused on cheap programming. 'In those days,' he says, 'our cost of programming was Rs 30,000 per hour. Even when we did something ambitious like *Saanp Seedi*, we got UTV to make it for us at Rs 55,000 per episode.'

The formula of low-cost programming worked brilliantly and Zee was an instant success, making Indians aware that there was more to television than Doordarshan. Chandra planned new channels when he was hit by an unexpected development.

In October 1993, Li Ka Shing sold STAR to Rupert Murdoch.

According to Chandra, Murdoch also had very little time for India – in those days, everyone was focusing on the Chinese market. He only began looking at Zee seriously when he realized that of the twenty million homes STAR claimed to reach, twelve million were in India and they were not, strictly speaking, STAR TV homes. They were Zee TV subscribers.

So, Murdoch sent for Chandra. It was the beginning of a complicated relationship.

A fight to the finish

Murdoch is not keen on partners. So, when he heard of Zee's success, his first response was to try and buy the channel. Chandra refused but the two men seemed to get along and Zee organized Murdoch's first visit to India.

Then, Chandra and Murdoch began a series of collaborations. Murdoch bought 49 per cent of Asia Today, the Subhash Chandra company that had leased the transponder. Star (Murdoch had ditched the abbreviation style) and Zee jointly set up Zee Cinema and Murdoch became an investor in Chandra's Siticable venture. Chandra turned down an offer of $500 million for the rest of Asia Today but relations seemed amicable.

When did the problems begin?

Chandra seems to think that the tension started after the Indianization of Star Plus in 1996. His original agreement with Murdoch prevented Star from running its own Hindi channel. But when Star Plus entered the Hindi market, Chandra sued Star in London.

After that, it seemed like a fight to the finish. Murdoch's executives claimed that Chandra pulled every string to make life difficult for Star. There was pressure on its managers – many of whom were former government employees – to resign on the grounds that they could not seek private employment for several years after leaving government. A court even issued a warrant for Murdoch's arrest on an obscenity charge relating to a Star Movies telecast.

In 1998, Zee and Star finally settled the London case. They severed all links with each other and Chandra paid $180 million for Murdoch's share of Asia Today and Siticable.

Given that Murdoch had valued Asia Today at nearly $1,000 million in 1995, it seemed that Chandra had won a major victory. But he also nullified the agreement which prevented Star Plus from going all Hindi.

And that single negation ensured that it was Murdoch who really won in the long run.

The ratings game

Star India used its newly-won freedom to plan an all-Hindi channel, the centrepiece of which was, of course, *Kaun Banega Crorepati* (*KBC*) with Amitabh Bachchan. When *KBC* was a huge hit, Zee programmers believed that this was a flash in the pan. They were wrong. Star Plus rode *KBC*'s success brilliantly, ensuring at one stage, that all fifty of the top fifty programmes were Star Plus serials.

So, does Chandra think he made a mistake by walking away from the battle with Murdoch? Zee is now so far behind Star Plus that he might have been better off preventing Star from doing Hindi programming.

Chandra does not agree. 'Yes, Zee has problems,' he concedes. 'We were complacent and reactive. We took our viewers for granted. When that happens, anyone can beat you. If it wasn't Star Plus, it would have been somebody else.'

Zee has tried to address the programming problems. Three years ago, it introduced a completely new slate of programmes, most of which, unfortunately, sank without a trace. That was another mistake, Chandra says. 'You cannot suddenly stop all your serials and tell viewers that they were idiots to have watched them because now you're going to introduce much better programming. Until then, loyal viewers had been willing to give Zee the benefit of the doubt. But this was the last straw.'

I ask him about the common media perception that Zee does poor programming because it is unwilling to spend money on shows. He denies it. 'Take *Time Bomb*,' he says, 'we spent Rs 25 lakhs per episode. If somebody has a good idea, he can have Rs 50 lakhs per episode. But he must get me ratings.'

Which *Time Bomb* hadn't, I point out.

Yes, he says, a little sadly.

What most people miss in this ratings battle is that unlike other networks, Zee is not dependent on its flagship channel. 'We have twenty channels,' says Chandra, 'and nearly all of them make money. Zee TV only accounts for 20 per cent of our revenues. We have a presence in 106 countries where we are actively marketed. I agree that Zee should do better in the ratings, but this matters less to us than it would to Sony or Star.'

On the prowl, for more

What does Subhash Chandra actually 'do' *these days*? 'I'm not a manager,' he says shortly. 'I don't have the patience for it. I'm an entrepreneur. I know that I can create something from nothing.'

Now, he has created *DNA*, a subject that makes both interviewer and interviewee tread an extremely cautious path. Why's he doing it, I ask.

' The owners of Bhaskar are old family friends. Our chemistry is right. When they launched *Divya Bhaskar* in Gujarat in June 2003, we discussed a partnership. Then we agreed that we would enter Mumbai together. They would look after printing and distribution. And we would look after editorial and marketing. But the decision to come to Mumbai was only taken on 17 February 2005. The *Hindustan Times* was launching and we didn't want to wait too long.'

What next for *DNA*?

'Another edition in the next two years, probably in the south.'

And what next for Subhash Chandra?

' Multiplexes, more channels, that sort of thing. I am not just in the TV business. I am in the entertainment business. And as more opportunities come, I will grab them.'

Knowing him, I'm sure he will.

bikki oberoi

Vice Chairman & MD, East India Hotels

▲

Here are three things you may not know about Bikki Oberoi. One: despite our tendency to continue to think of him as the son of Rai Bahadur Mohan Singh Oberoi and his own seemingly inexhaustible energy, he is actually seventy-seven years old, only a couple of years or so younger than, say, A.B. Vajpayee.

Two: he is one of a handful of hotel proprietors who has his own name on the properties he owns. There is no Mr Sheraton, no Mr Regent, no Mr Hyatt and Cesar Ritz has been dead for decades. The Hiltons have some shareholding in the eponymous company and there is a Mr Marriot but in both cases, the portfolios include downmarket properties, motels and institutional catering. Bikki is almost the last of a diminishing breed: a hotelier who puts his own name on luxury properties.

And three: he did absolutely no work till he was thirty-two.

It is the last of these three things that usually makes people sit up and look quizzical. Can he really have done absolutely nothing till he was well into his thirties?

'Yes, it is true,' says Bikki Oberoi, only a little defensively, adding, almost inevitably, 'and I am not defensive about it.'

['We have created a luxury Indian hotel brand on par with the best.']

The no-work-till-thirty-two story is an integral part of the Bikki legend but because he hardly ever gives interviews about his own life, nobody gets to ask him about it. But now that he's indicated that he is willing to discuss his playboy years, I seize the opportunity. What did he actually do till he was thirty-two?

Bikki Oberoi gives me one of those in-for-a-penny-in-for-a-pound looks. 'Well, I travelled,' he says. 'I spent a lot of time in London. I saw the world.'

Bit by bit, the story comes tumbling out. By the time Bikki was in his twenties, the Rai Bahadur had already made his fortune and established himself as a hotelier of some consequence. Clearly he indulged Bikki. But he also realized that to be a great hotelier you needed to experience the world's great hotels. And though he travelled a fair amount himself, he recognized the importance of letting his son sample the world's greatest hotels.

So Bikki went to London and stayed at the Savoy and at Claridges. He went to Paris and tried the Crillon. He went to New York and made his home at Carlyle. He went to Rome and loved the Hassler. He ate at the best restaurants. He drank the finest wines. He hung around with what was still called the jet set in the 1950s and 1960s.

The Rai Bahadur did not mind at all. In fact, he encouraged Bikki to travel. For instance, in 1956, he suddenly said to him, 'You know, I think that Japan is going to recover from the war defeat. Why don't you go there and see what it is like?'

So, Bikki went to Japan.

Of course, in those days, you couldn't just take a jumbo jet from Calcutta to Tokyo. Bikki flew first to Rangoon where he stayed at the Strand. From there he went to Bangkok – 'the airport was just a converted hangar', he recalls – where he stayed at The Oriental, in the days when the whole hotel consisted of just the Author's Wing. From Bangkok to Singapore and a few days at Raffles. Then, on to Hong Kong and the Peninsula Hotel before arriving in Tokyo where he stayed at the old Imperial Hotel.

He was very impressed by Japan, struck by the refusal of every single person to accept a tip – 'even if you tried forcing it on them' – and predicted that by the 60s, the country would be back in the reckoning.

' But the interesting thing for me,' he remembers, 'was how different the world was in those days. Bangkok was a small town. Singapore was not at all impressive. Hong Kong had yet to become a commercial capital. The two most impressive cities I saw on that journey were Calcutta, where I started out from, and Rangoon. Who would imagine that in this day and age?'

One consequence of all this travelling – when it was still a very big deal for Indians to go abroad – was that by the time he was thirty-two, Bikki was probably the most sophisticated man in the country. He had been everywhere. He had done everything. And even if he still hadn't learnt how to run great hotels, he had learnt how to enjoy them – from the perspective of a guest.

Building international properties

By the early 1960s, the Rai Bahadur was India's greatest hotelier with properties in Simla, Delhi (the Imperial and the Maidens), Calcutta and even, Pakistan. But it was the era of the global chains. Conrad Hilton had opened a hotel in Puerto Rico and had then built hotels all over the Third World. Pan Am, then America's premier airline, owned the Intercontinental chain and was keen on building a hotel in every capital.

The Rai Bahadur decided that he was going to open a modern five-star hotel and built the shell of his property in several acres of greenery at the edge of the Delhi Golf Club. But, because no foreign exchange was available in those days, he discovered he could not complete it.

He flew to Washington to look for solutions and asked B.K. Nehru, then India's ambassador to the US, if he could help. B.K. Nehru had an idea. If the Oberois found an American partner, they could get cheap financing from the US Exim Bank and access to PL 480 funds. The Rai Bahadur promptly tied up with Intercontinental and in the autumn of 1965, he opened the Oberoi Intercontinental, the first Indian hotel built on the lines of a modern international property.

It was at that stage that Bikki began to gradually involve himself in the business. He had contributed ideas to the conception of the Intercontinental and then, when his father planned his next big project, a hotel in Bombay's Nariman Point, he was fully involved in the planning of what became the Oberoi Sheraton. (The American collaborator was necessary for the Exim Bank financing, once again.)

By the end of the 1970s, even though the Taj had opened in Delhi and Madras, there was no doubt that the Oberoi was India's pre-eminent chain. Not only were there successful properties at home (the Bombay hotel was almost a licence to print money), but there were hotels abroad too: in Egypt, the Middle East and even Bali, long before the other international chains got there.

As the Oberois became an international chain and tied up with international collaborators, Bikki's travelling years suddenly began to seem more and more useful. A decade of being an international playboy had actually ended up being – as his father had probably anticipated – an invaluable research and development experience.

That's the great thing about the hotel business. You can enjoy yourself – and feel worthy doing it.

If you listen to Bikki talk about the Oberoi group, you realize how much he still hero-worships his father. He will tell all the old stories again – about how the Rai Bahadur got the Grand in Calcutta, about how he launched the first corporate take-over in Indian history in 1942; about how, during the Second World War, he toured India buying up all the Scotch because he knew there would soon be a shortage etc. – but he will always play down his own role in the success of the Oberoi group.

But the truth is that as remarkable as the old man was, the reason why the Oberois are India's classiest hotel chain today is: Bikki.

By the mid-1980s, the Oberois were still among the big boys on the block. But they were no longer the pre-eminent group. By most measures, the Taj, with two hotels in Delhi, two in Bombay, two in Madras, two in Bangalore, one under construction in Calcutta, great palaces in Rajasthan and a resort complex in Goa, was ahead of the Oberois. The new ITC chain was making rapid strides – a source of some chagrin since Bikki had helped plan the first ITC hotel, the Mughal in Agra, which was supposed to have been managed by the Oberois till ITC's Ajit Haksar decided to create his own chain. Plus, it was only a matter of time before the international chains made it to India with stand-alone properties.

Bikki's masterstroke was to take the Oberoi chain even further upmarket. Till then, everybody – the Rai Bahadur, the Taj's Ajit Kerkar etc. – had been content to build Hilton-Sheraton style international hotels.

But Bikki had been travelling. And he'd realized that the hotel business had changed. Once there had been the grand hotels and the chain hotels. But now, he realized, there was a third category: the upmarket chain hotel. This was at least one grade (and many dollars in room rates) above the Hilton-Sheraton kind of properties and offered a higher standard of luxury. It prided itself on service and on making the guest feel that he was special – not just yet another customer-in-a-room factory.

In 1986, Bikki opened the Oberoi in Bombay, next to the old Oberoi Sheraton (renamed Oberoi Towers after Sheraton went and tied up with ITC) and rewrote the rules of the game.

My sense of the hotel then was that it was heavily influenced by the upmarket Far Eastern Regent chain and Bikki now freely concedes that Bob Burns, who founded Regent, was his inspiration. With its butler service, its air of exclusivity (non-hotel guests were discouraged from entering the lobby), its granite floors ('only because we weren't allowed to import marble' he explains now) and its super-expensive Rotisserie restaurant, the Oberoi raised the bar for all Indian luxury hotels.

Next Bikki turned his attention to Delhi, where the old Oberoi Intercontinental (now called just the Oberoi) had been beaten by the Taj. He took the hotel so upmarket that the Taj was left far behind. It was an ugly building, a 1960s tower block with smallish rooms but Bikki redecorated the public areas, added new restaurants and raised the service standards so much that it became – and still remains – Delhi's most refined hotel.

Other properties – including the Grand in Calcutta – got the same treatment and when he opened new city hotels, such as the Oberoi Bangalore, the market took it for granted that he would build hotels that were the equivalent of Regent or Four Seasons properties rather than Intercontinentals or Sheratons.

By the early 1990s, Bikki was something of a legend in the hotel business. His critics had sneered that he was pitching his hotels too high – but now they had to eat their words. Those who saw him as a playboy without the patience to run a company were gobsmacked as he worked impossibly long hours, immersing himself in the business with a management style that was almost obsessively hands-on.

He was ready now to build the hotels for which he will probably be most remembered.

Exotic resorts

Bikki told the story of how the first Vilas property was built at the HT's Luxury Conference in January 2006. He was in Jaipur looking for a haveli to buy for himself (he ended up buying the Naila Fort eventually) and had to stay at the Rambagh Palace, owned by part of the Jaipur royal family (but not by Bikki's friend, Bhawani Singh, the Maharaja). 'I took my own servant. I took my own cook. I even took my own toilet paper,' he said. But he hated the Rambagh so much that he decided to build his own hotel in Jaipur. (To be fair, he did not name the Rambagh, but everybody who has heard Bikki's anecdotes knew which hotel he meant.)

The full story is a little more complicated. One of the gaps in the Oberoi portfolio was the resort segment. The Taj group had opened up Rajasthan (with the Rambagh and the Lake Palace) and created Goa as a destination. But the Rai Bahadur had focused on building city hotels – generally a surer source of profit than resort properties.

But Bikki wanted to build resorts. Only, he wanted to build world-class resorts. He admired Adrian Zecha of Aman resorts and his travels in the Far East had made him conscious of how second-rate Indian resort properties were. His idea was to build a sprawling resort in Jaipur that fused the décor themes of his Naila Fort with the elegance of a property in Bali or Phuket. When he bought land on the Jaipur-Agra road, miles away from the city centre and the monuments, others in the group told him he was crazy.

But Bikki knew what he was doing. He used designers with experience of East Asia to build Bali-style villas (with magnificent bathrooms, complete with sunken bath-tubs and glass walls that overlooked gardens) and opted for a spectacular Rajasthani fort-style main building. He made his son Vikram the first general manager and intensively trained a young and enthusiastic staff.

Because he was conscious that his competition was a real palace – the Rambagh – he decided not to use the Oberoi name and called the hotel Rajvilas or the Royal Apartments.

Almost from the day it opened, Rajvilas set new standards for the hotel industry in India. Because Bikki had counted on high room rates, which Indians were reluctant to pay, the economics of the property would only work if he could attract high-spending foreigners – and yet, everybody knew that rich foreign tourists overflew India on their way to East Asia.

As the scepticism mounted, Bikki continued to open Vilas after Vilas. Udayvilas, the most expensive of the lot, opened in Udaipur, Amarvilas, overlooking the Taj, became Agra's finest hotel; Vanyavilas, Bikki's personal favourite, opened near the Ranthambore sanctuary and Wildflower Hall became an English country house-style vilas in the hills above Simla.

Unfortunately for Bikki, the Vilas properties opened during bad years for Indian tourism. And because he did not get the rates he needed, his critics wondered if he had bet the whole company on hotels that would never make money.

Then, around three years ago, tourism began to pick up. And this year has been the best since the Vilas properties opened. All city hotels are full – but that is because of business traffic. The Vilases on the other hand have finally attracted the well-heeled tourists India never used to get. Many of the Vilas hotels now routinely appear on lists of the world's best hotels. And in both Jaipur and Udaipur, they are the prestige properties, beating the real palaces – the Rambagh and the beautiful, historic Lake Palace.

The guest is always right

The day I journey to the Oberoi farm, past Delhi's international airport, to meet Bikki Oberoi, he is busy composing a letter of apology to a guest. There is a rule at all Oberoi hotels that serious letters of complaint are to be forwarded to the chairman. The general manager of one of the Vilas properties (I will be discreet and not name the hotel) has sent Bikki an angry letter from a Hong Kong-based guest.

According to the letter writer, he was treated appallingly. They lost his reservations, gave him the wrong fax number, screwed up the morning alarm, could not find him a good table at the restaurant etc. etc.

Bikki is seriously perturbed. 'I always tell my staff that only one out of every ten guests who has a genuine complaint bothers to complain. I know that if I have a bad experience at a hotel or with an airline, I just resolve never to stay there again or switch to another airline. It is just too much trouble to complain. So, if somebody complains, it means he feels very strongly. And there are at least nine other people with similar experiences who have not complained.'

Bikki thinks the letter-writer – who has written to the hotel and not the chairman – has a genuine grievance. He writes him a personal letter apologising on behalf of the Oberois. He refunds the guest's entire bill amount. And he offers him four days' free stay at any Oberoi hotel of his choice.

Isn't that a bit excessive? I ask.

'Oh no. In this business, advertising and marketing only work up to a point. What really matters is word of mouth. So if you have got it wrong, you have to make it up to the guest as quickly as possible. There is no point being arrogant,' he says.

Bikki Oberoi thinks that there is no point being arrogant?

He laughs. He is not unfamiliar with his own reputation as a somewhat Napoleonic figure. 'When you are in a service business,' he states flatly, 'the guest is always right.'

Bikki has been planning a new Bangalore hotel. He is trying to get the architect of a new Gurgaon hotel (an Oberoi rather than the existing Trident) to put a small garden outside each room. He is overseeing the design of a new Nile Boat. He is giving the finishing touches to a new Vilas near Khajuraho. There is land in Goa and he is considering whether the market can take a luxury property – normally he is very disparaging about Goa, which, he believes, has gone too downmarket as a destination because of charter flights.

In the middle of these grand plans, he still finds the time to write personal letters of apology.

'Yes,' he says. 'I am very hands-on. You have to be. That is the nature of the business.'

It is a slightly unkind thing to say – especially since his father lived to be over 100 years old – but surely at seventy-seven, he must feel he has entered the twilight of his career?

He says yes, but everything about the way in which he behaves suggests the opposite. He still wants to build another hotel in Delhi. He thinks that the older Oberoi hotels are dated because the rooms are too small for genuine luxury properties. His dream, he says, is to pull down the Delhi Oberoi and build a new hotel on the same location.

The old Oberoi Sheraton in Mumbai is now called the Hilton Towers, part of a marketing deal Bikki has struck with the Hilton chain to rebrand his mid-priced properties.

I can understand him regarding his Trident hotels as mid-priced. But why the Nariman Point Towers?

Well, he says, there is the upmarket Oberoi next door and it was getting very confusing maintaining the branding if both hotels used the Oberoi name. By using the Hilton brand for the Towers, he has preserved the cachet of the Oberoi's luxury image.

That's funny, I say. In the days when his father and he struck deals with Intercontinental and Sheraton and worried about the competition from Hilton when it did come to India, did he ever conceive of a situation where the Oberoi brand would be too upmarket to be associated with the Hilton name?

' No,' he says, thoughtfully, ' But that is one thing I am proud of having done. We have created a luxury Indian hotel brand on par with the best.'

There's a Four Seasons opening in Mumbai, I say. Will his Oberoi finally be trumped?

Bikki Oberoi sits up. 'We are renovating The Oberoi,' he declares. ' And when we are through, it will be a better hotel than the Four Seasons. That is my challenge. And you will see how we do it.'

So not just better than Hilton, but better than Four Seasons as well?

'Oh yes,' he says. ' Otherwise, there's no point being in this business.'

nusli wadia

Chairman, Wadia Group of Companies

▲

His wife has, famously, described him as a 'crisis junkie', but that's not how Nusli Wadia likes to think of himself. He frowns a little when I remind him of the description and says, 'That's very frivolous. And it's not true.'

What about the charge that he loves a good fight so much that when there are no opportunities for combat in his own life, he scours the country looking for other people's conflicts?

'I have never looked for a fight,' says Wadia flatly. 'It is true that I have often had to fight but every one of these fights has been forced on me. It has not been of my own choosing.'

The most famous of these battles is, of course, the one that dominated headlines for all of the 1980s and much of the 1990s: Nusli Wadia vs Dhirubhai Ambani. It was a battle that spilled out of the boardrooms and ultimately became the centrepiece of Indian politics during the Rajiv Gandhi era. Many people still believe that the Rajiv Gandhi-V.P. Singh war was a by-product of the Wadia-Ambani feud. And certainly, Wadia has never been far from the political action; not in those days and not now, when he remains the only man in India with equal access to both the Vajpayee and Advani households.

[
'... I am not really a businessman.
It doesn't interest me that much.
Making money does not fascinate me.'
]

But the battle few people remember is the one that shaped Nusli Wadia's destiny. If he had lost it, he would not be sitting here today, in his spacious office in the compound of the Bombay Dyeing Mill in central Mumbai. He might not even be living in India at all.

It was the battle for his inheritance. And his opponent was his own father.

The first fight

The Wadias are one of India's most distinguished business families. But like the other great Parsi houses (among them, the Tatas and the Godrejs), they have always prided themselves on doing business honestly, on never paying bribes, and on never dealing in black money.

Neville Wadia, Nusli's father, was one of the great textile magnates of the old school. He was famous for the quality of his products – in those days, Bombay Dyeing was India's largest textile company – and as famous for his interest in philanthropy. But, by the 1960s, he had worked out that India was becoming a very different kind of place and that men like him, who insisted on doing business by the book, were an endangered species.

He negotiated to sell Bombay Dyeing to the Goenkas of Calcutta – R.P. Goenka handled most of the negotiations – and intended to go and settle in Switzerland. Aware that his only son, Nusli, might not take kindly to the idea, he conducted the negotiations in secret and the first Nusli heard of the sale was when a friend woke him up one morning and asked, 'I say, what's this I read in the papers about your father having sold Bombay Dyeing?'

Nusli was famously hotheaded. His parents had sent him to public school in England (Rugby) where, from all accounts, he was a bit of a failure. He came back to India, interrupting his studies, and was put to work on the shop floor. To everyone's surprise, he proved to be an astute and imaginative businessman and his major contribution to Bombay Dyeing was the introduction of the retail shops (in those days, most mills sold to wholesalers) and the development of the brand name.

But even as Nusli was learning to love the business, his father was tiring of the travails of running a mill in India. Selling out to a canny Marwari seemed like the best option for a Parsi gentleman of the old school. Neville intended to take the money and to live the life of a retired European aristocrat in a Swiss resort.

He had reckoned on Nusli's opposition but had underestimated his son's determination – and his ability to win allies. Though father and son were friendly, few people disputed that Nusli regarded J.R.D. Tata as an alternate father figure. The young Nusli spent much of his time with India's greatest living industrialist, learning his methods and understanding his philosophy.

So, the second call that Nusli got on the fateful morning that the newspapers reported the Bombay Dyeing sale was from J.R.D. Tata. 'You're not going to let him sell Bombay Dyeing, are you?' his mentor asked.

No, said Nusli, not if he could help it. But he wasn't sure how he could stop his father.

He hadn't counted on JRD's help. Together, they worked out a strategy whereby Nusli won the support of every executive and every worker on the Bombay Dyeing rolls. Lawyers opined that Neville did not have the right to sell the Wadia family's shares unilaterally. Armed with all this ammunition, Nusli took a flight to London to confront his father who was sitting in the English capital contemplating a happy and peaceful retirement.

He will never forget, says Nusli now, that when he sank into his First Class seat on the plane to London, there was a rose waiting for him on the armrest. Attached to the rose was a note from JRD, wishing him luck and promising him support. (JRD was chairman of Air India, which, I suppose, helped when it came to placing roses on seats.)

Nusli went from Heathrow to meet his father. The two men had an angry and stormy confrontation. Neville told Nusli that it was impossible to do business honestly in India. 'Don't be so immature,' he told his son, 'let's just take the money. We can live like lords in Switzerland.'

This had the effect of making Nusli even angrier. 'You can live in Switzerland,' he told the old man. 'I don't want to be a second-class citizen in some European country. I am going to live in India. And I am going to run Bombay Dyeing.'

Faced with a revolt of this magnitude, Neville gave in. The Goenkas were told that the deal was off. Nusli found new investors in the years ahead (among them the Scindias of Gwalior) and Bombay Dyeing continued to do better and better. By the mid-70s, Nusli was firmly in control and the old man was spending most of his time in his beloved Switzerland.

Nusli Wadia (with a little help from J.R.D. Tata) had won his first major battle.

The Dhirubhai tangle

But, of course, the old man was right. It was becoming more and more difficult to do business honestly in India. By the late 1970s, Bombay Dyeing was still the biggest and best textile company in India. But it was no longer the one that everyone talked about. That distinction went to Reliance whose founder-Chairman Dhirubhai Ambani made no secret of his ability to transform political and bureaucratic contacts into profits.

Though he is reluctant to repeat this now, Nusli Wadia used to claim, in the 1980s, that for Dhirubhai, it wasn't enough that Reliance succeeded. It was as important to make sure that everybody else failed. Wadia believed that the Ambanis did everything possible to throttle Bombay Dyeing, from nearly sabotaging his DMT project to ensuring that all government permissions went against the Wadias.

We talk now of the all-powerful Ambani machine, but in the early 1980s, when Wadia would complain about Reliance, most people thought he was being paranoid. He would say things like, 'You take my word; if Ambani is not stopped now, this man will become India's biggest industrialist. He has bought the whole system and manipulates everything.'

At that stage, Dhirubhai owned a successful textile company and not much else; so the notion that he would, one day, rub shoulders with the Tatas and the Birlas seemed laughable. The general view in the 1980s was that because Dhirubhai was a lot smarter than him, it suited Nusli to portray the Ambanis as all-powerful manipulators. That way, Nusli's own failure to compete effectively with Reliance could be explained away in terms of Dhirubhai's control of the government and the bureaucracy.

It may be a coincidence but nearly every other company that mattered in the textile sector in the 1980s – Baroda Rayon, Orkay, Nirlon, etc. – has either closed down or faces major problems. Would that have been the fate of Bombay Dyeing if Nusli had not enlisted the assistance of Ramnath Goenka and the *Indian Express*?

The way Nusli tells it now, the anti-Reliance campaign was Goenka's own idea. He was outraged that the Ambanis seemed to have more influence over the *Express* than he did himself and resolved to teach Dhirubhai a lesson. Moreover, says Wadia, in the early days at least, the campaign had the blessings of both, Prime Minister Rajiv Gandhi and Finance Minister V.P. Singh.

It was Wadia's idea – cleared, he says, with Rajiv Gandhi – to hire an American detective agency to investigate Reliance's purchase of a plant from Dupont, which the *Express* claimed, was subsequently smuggled into India. In those days, V.P. Singh's trusted director of enforcement was a man called Bhure Lal and he oversaw the investigation – keeping Rajiv briefed.

The problems began when, during one such briefing, in late 1986, Bhure Lal told Rajiv that he was investigating the illegal activities of many rich Indians, including the Bachchan brothers. Rajiv had never cleared any investigation of the Bachchans – this was V.P. Singh's own agenda to rid himself of a rival in Allahabad.

Then, Wadia later learnt, the Indian embassy in Switzerland reported that somebody had hired a detective agency to check on any bank accounts held by Rajiv or the Bachchans. As far as he knows, says Wadia, nobody had hired such an agency; this was pure misinformation.

But the smoking gun took the form of two sloppily forged letters allegedly written by the head of the American detective agency (Fairfax) investigating Reliance and addressed to Bhure Lal. In the letters, the agency referred to its investigations into the bank accounts of the Bachchan brothers and Sonia Gandhi's family in Italy. In retrospect, the letters looked like obvious forgeries – even at the time, many journalists, including myself, wrote that they were forgeries – but they had a dramatic effect when they were handed to Rajiv.

Here, at last, was confirmation of what the Ambanis had long been suggesting: V.P. Singh and Ramnath Goenka were not targeting Dhirubhai Ambani alone. The real target was Rajiv Gandhi.

Meets Rajiv finally, but ...

Everybody knows what followed. Rajiv became suspicious of Goenka. The press baron responded by attacking Rajiv. V.P. Singh was pilloried within the Congress and then left to start his own political party. The *Express*, with V.P. Singh's assistance, forced Amitabh Bachchan out of politics on trumped-up charges.

Nusli made several attempts to meet Rajiv but was never granted an audience. The Ambanis were suddenly back in favour. The entire might of the Indian State came down on Nusli Wadia. He was raided and then arrested in humiliating circumstances. Two burly policemen handcuffed him and led him out of the house. 'When will my Daddy come home?' Nusli's thirteen-year-old son asked one of the cops. 'He's going to jail for at least five years,' the policeman responded, causing the boy to burst into tears. Then, the Government of India served a deportation order on Wadia, who held a British passport in those days. The *Express* nearly went bankrupt. Bombay Dyeing went into a tailspin.

Nobody – well, almost nobody – did well out of that confrontation. V.P. Singh's opposition and the *Express* campaign led to the Bofors charges – which ultimately proved to be bogus – gaining a false credibility with the educated elite. And ultimately, Rajiv lost an election he deserved to win.

Nusli did not get to meet Rajiv Gandhi again till May 1991. They met for half an hour and Rajiv said, ' Nusli, I only wanted to help you. Why did you damage me so much?' Nusli retorted, ' What about all the things your government did to me?'

They met again a week later. Nusli went to 10 Janpath at 10 p.m. He left at 5 a.m. The two men spent most of the night sorting out the misconceptions and the misunderstandings. History could not be rewritten. But perhaps the mistakes of the past could be avoided.

They parted, Nusli recalls, having understood each other better. They promised to meet once the election campaign was over.

A fortnight later, Rajiv was dead.

The cookie lures

The 1990s were a crucial decade for Nusli Wadia. It is a cruel thing to say but by then, he was no longer a major preoccupation for the Ambanis: they were now so big that they had simply outgrown him. But while the Reliance juggernaut rolled on, Wadia had to prove that he knew how to run a business. He had to pick up the pieces at Bombay Dyeing and he had to demonstrate that he could grow the family empire.

Rebuilding the textile business proved tricky but an investment in Bombay Burmah yielded a gold mine in terms of hidden assets. And then, there was the cookie affair.

Nusli had always dreamt of entering the biscuit business and had negotiated with the ailing Huntley and Palmer biscuits to take over Britannia in India. But Huntley and Palmer itself was taken over by American cookie giant Nabisco and though Nusli met the Nabisco brass through his friend (and partner in a cashew company), Rajan Pillai, and seemed to have struck up a deal whereby he would still get to buy Britannia, the Americans later changed their minds. They kept Britannia and installed as chairman, not Nusli Wadia, but Rajan Pillai. (By then, the two men had fallen out over the cashew company and were no longer speaking to each other.)

Eventually, Nabisco too was taken over and through a series of complex, possibly backdated, agreements, Rajan Pillai emerged as the new owner of Britannia. Pillai took the French group Danone as his partners but the two soon fell out with Danone accusing Pillai of cheating.

Re-enter Nusli, this time as Danone's new Indian partner. After a bruising legal and media battle, Pillai was ousted and Wadia finally got his heart's desire: control of Britannia. It is a company that has grown rapidly and today, with a market capitalization of around Rs 2,000 crore and a profitability of Rs 175 crore, it does better than Bombay Dyeing. (Though, of course, Bombay Dyeing has many undervalued assets, including the land it sits on.)

The Britannia acquisition demonstrated that not only did Nusli know how to fight a good fight – he also knew how to make a profit at the end of it.

The saffron link

Nusli Wadia's detractors never tire of pointing out that he is M.A. Jinnah's grandson (his mother is Jinnah's daughter). Nusli is not embarrassed by his lineage; in fact, he's very proud of Jinnah, who he regards as having been entirely secular. The Partition, he says, was an unfortunate event but the Congress must share the blame.

But it is odd, isn't it, that Jinnah's grandson should be so close to the BJP?

Since the 1960s, when the Jan Sangh was a party of petty shopkeepers, Wadia has been a dedicated fellow traveller. He still idolizes Nanaji Deshmukh and both A.B. Vajpayee and L.K. Advani have been his friends for years. When the BJP finally took office, he was a key member of the government's inner circle.

Nusli doesn't see any contradiction in his lineage (Muslim-Parsi) and his friendship with the party of Hindutva. He says that he was drawn to the Jan Sangh because he believed that India needed an opposition party that believed in free markets. He is not, he concedes, a great believer of Hindutva.

Even so, I ask, wasn't he embarrassed by the demolition of the Babri Masjid?

'Of course, I was,' he responds. 'I don't believe in any kind of religious extremism. That's not what politics is about.'

I press him on his closeness to the last government. Is it true that he was one of the two or three men who knew that Advani was going to be made deputy prime minister?

He does not deny it.

Is he embarrassed then, I ask, by the revelations that the war between the Ambani brothers have thrown up. Isn't it odd that a party which counts Nusli as part of its inner circle should have been so successfully penetrated by the Reliance machine that telecom policy was rewritten at Nariman Point?

Nusli is normally a voluble – opinionated even – sort of fellow. But now, he falls strangely silent.

I push further. Well, what do these revelations say about his beloved BJP's desire to clean up Indian industry?

He finally responds. 'I would rather not comment,' he says.

Politics yes, politician no

I've interviewed Nusli Wadia before and written about him several times. But here's the thing: not one of these stories has been about business. He has the rare distinction of being the businessman who has been the most involved in Indian politics over the last two decades. (With the possible exception of Dhirubhai Ambani, I suppose ...)

But with the BJP out of power and in disarray, Nusli finally has a business focus to his life. Bombay Dyeing is doing well: the textile business is still rocky but the real estate division is performing brilliantly. Britannia is a bonafide success. And now, his son's plans to launch a low-cost airline by the autumn of 2005 have been successful.

I ask him about the rumours that he was never keen on the airline. 'Nonsense,' he explodes. 'I am totally behind the project. We are putting our family money into the airline, around Rs 50 crore or so. It is not coming out of Bombay Dyeing.'

But does he see himself as a businessman?

'Yes,' he says thoughtfully. 'I suppose I am a businessman.' He pauses. 'But I am also not really a businessman. It doesn't interest me that much. Making money does not fascinate me.'

The obvious question: Why hasn't he joined politics?

'Because I don't want to stand for election and all that,' he says shortly. 'Last year there was a rumour that I was being nominated to the Rajya Sabha and it annoyed me so much that I didn't go to Delhi till the nominations were announced.'

And the final, slightly rude, question. For two decades now, it has been almost impossible to think of Nusli without thinking of the Ambanis. Now, that their paths seem finally to have diverged, does he still harbour them any ill will?

Nusli answers carefully. 'I never wanted the Ambanis to be part of my life. It was never my choice. And if we have nothing to do with each other now, I'm quite happy with that.'

And it shows.

uday kotak

Vice Chairman and MD, Kotak Group of Companies

▲

A single statistic should help put Uday Kotak's success in perspective. In 1986, when he started his business, he borrowed money from family and friends to collect the Rs 30 lakh that he put into the company. If you had been a friend of Uday Kotak's during that period and if you had enough faith in him to have invested in his business, then you would be a very rich man today.

If you had put Rs 1 lakh into Uday's business, your stake would be worth Rs 100 crore today.

Not bad going, eh?

There are great financial success stories in America and Europe. The great names of finance – Rothschild, J.P. Morgan, Goldman Sachs, etc. – were all individuals who went into financial services of one kind or another and created empires that have outlasted them.

But try as I might, I cannot think of a single parallel outside of Europe and America that matches what Uday Kotak has achieved in the Indian financial market. Almost by definition, there are no such stories in the world of high finance in Africa. China has a State-controlled economy. And in the rest of Asia, it's the international firms that dominate the finance markets.

[

'... if what you create cannot outlive you,
then I think, you have failed.'

]

Only in India, do we have a Uday Kotak, a man who came out of nowhere and in less than two decades, not only made a massive fortune but also created a financial brand that will probably outlast him just as J.P. Morgan has outlasted Pierpont Morgan.

It is something that Uday is understandably proud of. As he told Anand Mahindra, an early investor in his business, ' Let's put our names into the company. All the great financial houses – the Morgans, the Rothschilds and the others – are known by the names of their founders. Let's show people that we care enough about this business to put our names on it.'

Mahindra agreed and today, his stake in the business (owned personally, not through Mahindra and Mahindra) is worth hundreds of crores. But even he must never have imagined that, in under twenty years, Uday's company would have a market cap of Rs 6,700 crore or that he would run the third-largest private sector bank in India.

Cricket and calculus

Uday describes his background as middle class. But his family was – by any standards – comfortably upper-middle class. They were traditional Gujarati cotton traders who diversified into other commodities.

When Uday was born, they all lived together in a large house in Babulnath (next to the temple) where sixty family members shared a single kitchen. Then, Uday's father and uncle moved out to Laburnum Road, a sleepy, leafy Gujarati-dominated area just off Hughes Road. (Kotak Kunj on Hughes Road belongs to another branch of the same family.) Though the family were of the right background to have sent their son to Cathedral, Campion or any of the other top schools of the 1960s, they chose a rather obscure institution called Hindi Vidya Bhavan on Marine Drive because the school had been inaugurated by Morarji Desai and the Kotaks believed in its nationalist principles.

When he was at school, Uday discovered that he had two great talents. The first was cricket – he eventually became captain of the school team and went on to play in the Kanga League when he joined college.

But it was the second talent that was to determine the course of his life. He wasn't just good at math, he seemed to have a special relationship with figures. Numbers spoke to him. He could look at a sum and suddenly it made more sense to him than it did to any of his classmates.

He did well enough in school to get into Sydenham for a four-year B.Com course. In the first year, he was among the top students in Bombay University. But by the third year, he had hit his stride. He topped the university, a feat he was to repeat in his final year.

The logical thing for him to have done was to join the family business, but he decided that he wanted an MBA first. He applied to only one school – Bajaj in Bombay – and naturally, he was selected at once. He enjoyed Bajaj, he says. He played competitive cricket, he topped his class.

And oh yes, he nearly died.

Brush with death

It happened this way. In September 1979, he was playing cricket in the Kanga League, thwacked the ball and went for a run. He doesn't remember how, but presumably a fielder threw the ball back to the stumps and somehow, it hit Uday on the head.

He crumpled into an unconscious heap on the pitch and was rushed to hospital. The doctors told his parents that he had had a brain hemorrhage and that there was no hope. Nevertheless, they operated instantly.

Looking back, he says, it was the decision to operate within two hours of the injury that saved his life. Had they waited, there would certainly be no Kotak Mahindra today.

Against the odds, Uday survived, but because he took a while to recover from the operation, he missed a semester at Bajaj. Finding himself with nothing to do during this period, he began going to the office of the family business in the Navsari building in the Fort.

It was not a happy experience, though he says that it was a huge lesson for him. 'For every decision, I had to deal with fourteen family members and the one thing it taught me was to never do business with family. We have 5,000 employees at Kotak today and not one of them is related to me.'

By the time he was finally finished with Bajaj, he decided to give the cotton business a miss and was all set to join Hindustan Lever. Naturally, his father was appalled. He consulted other family members, all of whom had been impressed by Uday's financial skills, and they agreed to give him an office space of 300 square feet within the Navsari building premises. Uday was now free to do his own thing though it was understood that his operation was still a branch of the larger family business.

This was fine with Uday because by now, his astute financial brain had sensed a huge opportunity.

Opportunity comes calling

In those days, remembers Uday, banks gave depositors a 6 per cent return on their money. But if a company went to the same bank to borrow funds, the banks charged an interest of 16.5 per cent.

Something about this spread did not sound right to Uday. Obviously, the banks were making too much money. And just as obviously, there was money to be made by anybody who could find a way of reducing this spread.

It was around this time that he met somebody who handled finance for Nelco, the Tata electronics company. Nelco needed working capital and Uday thought that this presented an opportunity. He spoke to associates and friends and asked if they would be willing to lend money to Nelco. He assured them a return that was higher than the 6 per cent the banks were giving. And he told Nelco that the interest would be lower than the bank rate. 'It worked,' he says, 'because we were dealing with a Tata company. Everybody I spoke to was willing to lend to a Tata company because the deposit was risk-free.'

From these relatively straightforward transactions, Uday

advanced into bill discounting, using the same principles. Next, he spotted another opportunity. In the early 1980s, many foreign banks with huge international assets had opened shop in India. Because of government regulations, these banks did not actually have that much money for their Indian operations. On the other hand, some of the older foreign banks – Standard & Chartered, for instance – had lots of cash and needed to find some use for it. So, Uday moved into arranging financing for the newer European banks. 'I didn't have to do much,' he recalls, 'it was all a question of getting a bill and getting the bank to put its *chhaapa* (stamp) on it.'

But it was a profitable business and he was soon making a few lakhs a year, which wasn't bad for a young man just out of business school. He sensed that he needed to expand and doubled his staff from three to six. The problem was that the size of the office remained the same, so he hit on an ingenious solution: 'We doubled the working area by cutting all the desks in half.'

The Mahindra magic

When he looks back on his life, Uday Kotak thinks that 1985 was probably one of the most significant years. That was when, on the advice of a friend and mentor, Sidney Pinto of Grindlays, he decided to start a professional business of his own. That was also the year he met his wife, Pallavi. It was practically love at first sight: they married within months. And it was the year that Anand Mahindra, whom he dealt with while arranging funds for Mahindra Ugine, told him that he would invest in any business that Uday wanted to start.

'Anand had just come back from business school in the US and he understood that the financial services revolution was certain to hit India. In early 1986, when the business took shape, Anand put four or five lakh into the company and his father agreed to be the chairman. We had an investment of Rs 30 lakh and I cast around desperately for investors and borrowed money to be able to buy my own stake,' Uday remembers. 'And with

Anand on board, we were able to call the company Kotak Mahindra like Goldman Sachs or one of the other big Western firms that I admired. And let's be honest. The Kotak name meant nothing. But the addition of Mahindra gave the company instant credibility.'

Despite these auspicious beginnings, Uday didn't move out of Navsari building till 1988 when, at the urging of Anand's father, Harish, he bought offices in Nariman Bhavan at Nariman Point. 'It was a big decision but looking back, it was crucial for us to have scaled up. We were making money from bill discounting. I had bought a stock market card and we were into equipment leasing which was a popular tax shelter,' he remembers.

In 1989-90, Citibank launched the car financing business in India. In those days, you had to wait six months or so if you wanted a car unless you were willing to pay a premium. Kotak entered the business but offered an added plus. Kotak Mahindra would buy many cars in its own name, so if you went to the company for a car loan, not only would you get financing but you would also get the car on the spot.

After that, the successes kept coming. At Anil Ambani's wedding, Uday ran into a friend who had a fixed deposit distribution business that he wanted to get rid of. Uday bought it off him for around Rs 50 lakh and got an 800 square feet office in Dalal Street as part of the deal. In 1991, Kotak Mahindra got into merchant banking and the profits were good.

In December 1991, the company went public and Uday felt he was on the road to creating the financial services institution he had always dreamt of.

The unsung story

In 1993, Uday went international. At a Euromoney conference in Delhi, he met people from Goldman Sachs and in his own words, 'I just *chipkoed* to them.' Goldman Sachs liked what they saw and Uday became friends with senior partner Hank Paulson. Two years later, Goldman Sachs signed a JV with Kotak for banking and securities. At around the same time, Mahindra and Mahindra launched a JV with Ford, so it was convenient for Kotak Mahindra to do its own JV with Ford Motor Credit, the company's car financing arm.

'All this was important for me,' says Uday, 'because till then I had no idea how global financial businesses were managed. Dealing with Goldman Sachs helped me learn how to run a financial business. It also taught me that things were changing very quickly in India – especially after the reforms – and that the old ways of doing business were dead. We had to adopt global norms.'

In 1998, he launched the Kotak Mutual Fund, which he saw as a logical extension in the financial services sector. By then, he had already done something unusual. But because he had done it so quietly, nobody really noticed.

Uday Kotak had become a press baron.

It was never his intention originally to buy *Business Standard*, he says. Like everybody else, he thought it was a damn good paper and was distressed when he realized that its owners, Kolkata's ABP Group, did not have the money to run it properly. 'At that stage,' he remembers, '*BS* was losing Rs 1.5 crore a month and there was a very real sense that ABP would be bankrupted by the losses. Aveek and Arup Sarkar came to me and said that they were desperate for a buyer.'

By then, ABP had spun *BS* off into a separate company but was still responsible for its losses. The idea was to find a rich man who would buy the new company. 'We went to all the usual names, the Ambanis, the Wadias, the Tatas, etc., and nobody was willing to buy it.'

As the desperate search yielded no results, Uday recalls, the Sarkars seemed ready to give up. 'Arup Sarkar told me in so many words that he could not afford to keep *BS* going. As no buyer had been found, they were simply going to close the paper down.'

Uday thought about it. The problem, as he saw it, was not that *BS* was a bad product – far from it. The problem was that there was an economic downturn and a big project like *BS* could not survive with small-time capital and financially strapped owners. 'I did a quick calculation. I believed that if I put Rs 20 crore into the paper, we could turn it around. The cost of acquisition was virtually zero. The Sarkars were so desperate that they were ready to give the paper up for nothing. I can't remember how much we paid but it was only a crore or so. Kotak Mahindra was flush with funds – some from the Goldman Sachs JV – so it seemed like a risk worth taking.'

He was wrong about one thing, he says, but right about the other. He was convinced that *BS* could only survive if T.N. Ninan, the paper's highly regarded editor, agreed to run the business. ' In the media business, you have to let journalists run the show because they understand what to do. If you interfere, try and impose management on them, or act as though you're some great press baron, you can never make a success of a media business,' he says. 'So, I removed myself from the actual running. T. Thomas, who got along with Ninan, chaired the board, and Ninan proved to be as talented a manager as he is an editor. It is because of Ninan that the paper makes profits today.'

So, what did he get wrong? 'I was too optimistic. The downturn lasted longer than I had expected. I ended up spending Rs 40 crore, not Rs 20 crore as I had thought. And we took on new investors from Great Eastern Shipping, who put in another Rs 20 crore. So, we spent Rs 60 crore, three times what I had planned. But,' he says, 'it was worth it because it's not just a profitable paper, it's also a very good paper.'

And, to his lasting credit, he pulled it off without ever letting the power of being a press baron go to his head.

Riding out the storm

The rest of the Kotak story reads like a list of successes. Once Uday had a certain critical mass, he just kept expanding. By the end of the 1990s, he was one of the most respected names in Indian finance and nearly every big deal came to his firm. Businessmen sought him out for financial advice and any foreigner seeking to invest big money in India rang his doorbell before proceeding further.

There was just one nervous moment. In 1997, as finance companies mushroomed all over India, Uday had an epiphany. He called in his senior managers and told them, 'I am willing to bet that in one year's time, 99 per cent of these finance companies will go bust. I want you to stop going out and looking for business. In fact, I want to shrink our lending by 50 per cent.'

It was a strange thing to say – but it was also the right thing to do. As credit was squeezed, the financial sector faced its biggest-ever crisis. Most finance companies did go bust, but Kotak rode out the storm. 'I told my people not to focus on return on equity but to just focus on equity. In other words, keep your capital in place,' he says. 'That's why we survived that phase with our net worth intact. We took a hit of Rs 100 crore in bad debts but by then, we were strong enough to manage.'

What made him do it? 'I think there are two sides to my personality. At one level, I like scaling up and I want to expand. But I am also a very conservative and cautious person. There is this constant conflict between these two contradictory personality traits. In this case, the conservative part of me won out. I kept thinking that if UTI was in trouble, the government would bail it out. But nobody was going to bail Kotak out. So, that paranoia probably saved us.'

Kotak is now into insurance and has massively expanded in banking. A branding exercise has concluded that the single name Kotak should be emphasized so that people are not confused by various Kotak companies. It seems to have worked. If, during his first decade, Uday Kotak won the confidence of India's top businessmen, he seems to have used the second decade to win the faith of India's consumers, who flock to his bank and his insurance company.

He is still only forty-six and has much of his working life ahead of him. His empire will surely grow as financial services assume a more central place in our economy. Did he ever imagine, I ask, that his skill with figures would lead him to this position?

' It's not the thing with numbers,' he replies. ' There are many people who are much better with figures than I am, even in my own company. Whatever I have achieved is due to three things. One: concentrate on substance not form. Two: believe in a value system, not just in profits. And three: recognize the importance of process over creativity. Because Indians are a creative people, we rely on discretion and instinct. But when you're building an institution, there is no substitute for process. That's what all my dealings with foreign companies have taught me.'

Is that his greatest success? That he could have been a multimillionaire, global financial wizard and deal-maker. But that he chose to create an institution instead?

' Yes, if what you create cannot outlive you, then I think, you have failed.'

fishing for more business:
the kingfisher way

vijay mallya
Chairman, UB Group

▲

V ijay Mallya provokes strong reactions. Among people who don't know him, he is seen as a glamorous jet-set figure, fond of fast cars, fast horses and the fast life. His wealth seems limitless. His interests tend to change from year to year. But no matter what he does, he spends a lot of money doing it.

People who do know him, however, are a little more judgemental. Despite the size of his empire and his undoubted success – about which, more later – he never quite gets the respect he deserves from the business community.

Some of this has to do with the very things that make him seem glamorous to outsiders. There is a strong tradition within Indian business of underplaying wealth. Partly, this is because the Indian rich are conscious of their privileged position within a poor country and do not wish to draw undue attention to their money. And partly, it is because the traditional business class regards conspicuous consumption as an essentially nouveau riche activity. The old rich don't flaunt their money; they let it speak for itself.

But some of the reservations that other business people have about Vijay emerge from the perception that he is essentially a

[
'I don't want to be Richard Branson.
I want to be Vijay Mallya.'
]

dilettante who flits from business to business, making a success of nothing in particular, but surviving because of the strength of the liquor empire that his father left him.

And, of course, some of it stems from his own personality. In a business environment where Anil Ambani – who does not smoke, drink or eat meat and whose idea of a glamorous leisure activity is to run a marathon – is regarded as flamboyant, nobody quite knows what to make of Vijay.

There is the jewellery to begin with. It is hard to think of an industrialist's wife who wears as much jewellery as Vijay does every day. Then, there's his entourage. Vijay is never alone. Wherever he goes, friends, employees and chamchas fly with him. Each evening, his living room feels like the location of a party that never ends. And when he talks, there is always the sense that he is addressing unseen multitudes behind your left shoulder.

All this makes other business people very uneasy.

But it also makes Vijay very happy.

Rich man's son

I don't think you can ever fully understand Vijay Mallya unless you understand the circumstances of his adolescence.

He was a rich man's son all right, but he was never brought up to feel rich. His father, the late Vittal Mallya was a low-profile billionaire who made his fortune in the liquor trade but never drew attention to his wealth.

When Vijay was a child, his parents separated and he moved to Calcutta (Kolkata now) with his mother. His father married again and started a new family in Bangalore. If anybody enjoyed the benefits of Vittal's wealth, it was this new family. Vijay, by his own admission, lived a fairly normal upper-middle-class existence. He would offer to fix people's cars to make extra pocket money and he remembers asking his father to bring him back a single pair of Levi's jeans from one of his trips abroad.

When I first interviewed Vijay about fifteen years ago, the story came tumbling out. How he longed for his father's approval.

How Vittal was physically affectionate when he met his young son but how he never made any commitments about inheritance. How Vijay, at some deep level, envied the Mercedes lifestyle of Vittal's new family. And how he never dreamt that he would be so rich one day.

These days, he is less keen to tell that story though, to be fair to him, he does not deny any of its essential components. Instead, he would rather focus on his own achievements than discuss the circumstances of his inheritance.

Vittal did finally give Vijay some inkling that he would be his successor – there were no sons in the new family – and he apprenticed him with many of his companies and then sent him to America for some on-the-job training.

Then, long before anybody thought Vijay was ready, Vittal died. At that stage, the UB empire was divided into many suzerainties, each with its own viceroy. Many of these people were Vittal's contemporaries and regarded Vijay as a brash young man without the talent or the experience to fill his father's shoes.

Vijay's first battle was to secure his own inheritance. One by one, the viceroys were either defeated or won over till Vijay was able to take charge of the empire. Then, eager to prove that he was not some idiot son who had hit the jackpot, he embarked on a series of investments, most of which were to end up as failures.

The ideas were all good; it was the execution that was lacking. He diversified into soft drinks but Thril, his cola, was a flop. He recognized the potential of fast food but his pizza chain failed because the pizzas themselves were disgusting.

Then he overreached himself. This was a time when Marwari businessmen were busy taking over foreign companies through the back door. Typically, they would find an NRI and ask him to buy out the foreign shareholding of an Indian company in his own name. Of course, the whole deal would be a benami transaction with the Marwari retaining effective control but because the laws had been amended to encourage NRI investment, the scheme was – on paper, at least – entirely legal.

Vijay approached Manu Chhabria (who was also negotiating to buy Dunlop in partnership with R.P. Goenka during this period) and worked out a scheme to buy R.G. Shaw, the foreign company that owned a controlling stake in Shaw Wallace, UB's principal competitor.

The deal went sour when the professional managers who ran Shaw Wallace put up a spirited defence. More to the point, they also alerted the enforcement authorities about Vijay's suspected role in the transaction.

Vijay and Chhabria were both raided. Because Chhabria was an NRI, he was beyond the purview of Indian lawmen. But Vijay had no such protection. He was harassed, interrogated and even arrested. As the pressure grew, he fell out with Chhabria and eventually, when the Shaw Wallace takeover did go through, Vijay had no stake in the company.

By the end of the 1980s with the fiascos of the Shaw Wallace takeover, the failed pizza business, the dud cola drink and the continual prosecutions of the enforcement authorities, it was beginning to seem as though things had gone very wrong for Vijay Mallya.

Perhaps, the viceroys had been right all along.

Global company

Vijay's response was to become an NRI. At a stroke, he rid himself of all the FERA problems and was beyond investigations of foreign dealings. But being Vijay, he did it in style. There was the massive country house in England and soon, there was a private plane, long before it became fashionable for Indian businessmen to run their own aircraft.

Then, Vijay turned his attention to foreign companies. He looked at Africa and bought into Berger Paints, arguing that he wanted to create the first Indian multinational. I remember talking to him about the scheme. Why, I asked, as politely as possible under the circumstances, would a man who had failed to sell pizzas to Indians imagine that he had it in him to create a global company?

Vijay's answer was logical. India's great strength, he said, was the skill of its managers. His plan was to buy undervalued international companies and to install Indian managers to run them. Given the talents of our home-grown professionals, these companies could be turned around at minimal cost. Once that happened, he would either run flourishing multinationals or sell out at a huge profit.

There was no denying the sense in what he said but even in those days, people who knew him well warned me, 'Vijay is a great talker. He can sell deep-freezers to Eskimos. The only problem is that he ends up believing his own bullshit.'

Such scathing assessments of his style were not uncommon in that era. Many of them stemmed from a mixture of envy and bemusement. Try and look at it from the perspective of the critics: here was this large, loud guy who had inherited a booze empire from one of the great, low-profile geniuses of Indian industry. Almost everything he had done in the 1980s and the early 90s had failed: colas, pizzas, the Shaw Wallace takeover, Mangalore Chemicals and God alone knows, what else. And yet, he was completely unfazed. His confidence was never dented. He spent money as though it was going out of style. He bought private planes, country houses and dozens of racehorses. How could Vijay possibly pull it off? Surely, something had to give.

And so, for much of the first half of the 1990s, the business community badmouthed Vijay and predicted his imminent demise. He was too disorganized, they said. He was incapable of turning up on time for a single appointment. He treated his employees like *chamchas*. (One particularly vicious story from that period, told to me by one of Vijay's contemporaries, had it that Mallya would invite senior managers to play tennis with him. As long as they lost, their careers were assured. But if they dared defeat him ...) The nasty speculation reached its height when Vijay's business rivals put it about that he was over-committed, deeply in debt, and unable or, perhaps, just unwilling to repay even small loans. As long as all this remained in the realm of gossip, Vijay acted as though he couldn't care less. But then, *Business Today* put him on the cover. The headline delivered the killer blow – 'Is Vijay Mallya going bust' – it asked.

Vijay was appalled, angered and upset. I met him in Bangalore just after the story appeared and though he tended to blame the piece on a one-time friend-turned-rival (now deceased), he was full of stories about how he had to phone every banker and business associate and assure them that the *Business Today* piece was not true and that he was far from bankrupt.

Gamble pays off

In retrospect, there is no doubt that Vijay was spending much more money than people thought he had. Worse still, in an era where Indian business still did not have a global outlook, he was spending this money in foreign currency. No wonder other businessmen thought he was overreaching himself.

But the critics made three crucial errors. First of all, they underestimated quite how profitable Vijay's liquor business was. No matter how his other companies did, the booze operations ensured that Vijay was always cash rich. Secondly, they did not realize quite how much of a risk-taker he was: this was an era, remember, when Indian businessmen tended to get their own money out of their projects even before the factories were erected. So, his rivals could simply not conceive of a man who was willing to put his money where his mouth was.

And third, nobody counted on another factor: Vijay Mallya is very lucky. No matter what he does, he always manages to land on his feet. His failures are quickly forgotten – by the rest of the world, but especially, by Vijay himself – while his successes tend to endure.

So even as the doubters were writing him off, Vijay was concentrating on a dozen other things. It was his ambition to turn Kingfisher beer into a global brand – an effort that even his critics will concede has been largely successful. He sensed an opportunity when the Chhabria brothers fell out and quickly linked up with Kishore Chhabria and partnered him for the successful Officer's Choice whiskey. (This venture ended in tears a decade later but at the time it had the effect of damaging Manu and Vijay was able to eventually walk away from the deal with no lasting damage.) Then, he developed a fascination with the media. He took over *Blitz*, obtained the franchise for the Bangalore edition of the *Asian Age*, invested in television and when his friend Ketan Somaaya suffered from financial difficulties, took over *Cine Blitz* (which later spawned *Hi Blitz*, a publication in which Vijay features prominently every month).

He was able to do all this because, far from the public eye, the liquor business was growing from strength to strength. Vittal had been conscious of the danger to the booze industry posed by pious, prohibition-loving politicians (he remembered how Morarji Desai had wanted to ban liquor in 1977) and believed that the future of his group lay in diversification. Vijay understood the argument for diversification but because he was a risk-taker, invested in increasing liquor capacity. It was a gamble that more than paid off as the profits shot sky-high.

Brand ambassador

By the beginning of this century, Vijay Mallya was a fact of life. He had made no attempt to moderate his lifestyle – in fact he had added homes in Manhattan, California and Goa. The horses won all the top races. The fast cars kept coming. The Versace shirts had given way to other trendier but equally flamboyant outfits. There were now more private planes, including a large Boeing 727, which he had customized so that his guests could jive and party all the way to their destinations.

When he was asked about the lifestyle, he even had a smart answer ready. He was in the business of promoting good times, he said. So, everything he did worked as publicity for the UB brand. In fact, he argued, he was doing it all for the company. He was Kingfisher's brand ambassador.

But even as the parties continued and the booze profits came rolling in, there was a sense in which Vijay was bored. He needed excitement that neither beer nor Black Dog (the world-famous Scotch whiskey brand that he owns) could provide. He had wearied of media, had tired of jetting around the world and had lost interest in creating Indian-owned multinationals.

Politics was the obvious next step. Vijay had always been friends with R.K. Hegde, the former chief minister of Karnataka. As the politics of Karnataka descended into bedlam, Hegde suggested to Vijay that he should enter public life. In fact, said Hegde, Vijay could be his designated successor.

To his credit, Vijay did not approach any of the existing parties, cap in hand. Instead, he created his own party. And when he needed a name, he linked up with Subramaniam Swamy who owned the legendary Janata Party name. Vijay's own election to the Rajya Sabha made possible by MLAs who shunned their own party candidates to vote for Mallya was not part of this enterprise. But once he entered Parliament, he sensed that this was something he wanted to do.

I interviewed him twice during this period. And while he gave the usual rhetorical answers ('I am doing this for the future of the children of India') there was no doubt that he genuinely believed that he had a real chance of wielding effective political power. His plan was as follows: with Karnataka politics in disarray, any new party stood a good chance of winning a substantial chunk of seats. These would not be enough for a majority. But in an era of minority governments, Vijay's party could well hold the balance of power.

For much of this decade, Vijay was obsessed with politics. He toured every corner of Karnataka (even risking his life when his helicopter crashed), bought Tipu Sultan's sword as a symbolic gesture, and acted as though he was on the cusp of success.

Alas, it was not to be. Most of his candidates lost their deposits though a couple of MLAs who had used his symbol in nearby Andhra did manage to get elected. A lesser man would have been devastated by the reverse. Vijay just put it behind him. 'We didn't have enough time to establish ourselves,' he says now. 'Despite being a new party, we still did very well. Maybe, we will do even better in the next election.' And, in any case, he still has his Rajya Sabha membership.

It is somehow typical of Vijay that even as his critics were dissecting the fiasco of his political career, the man himself was already on to the next big thing. When the aviation sector opened up, Vijay decided that he would run his own airline.

Kingfisher – he chose the brand as the airline's name – has been through many avataars. An early version was planned as a low-cost airline and his PR people put it about that Vijay would be the Richard Branson of India, given his beard and his flamboyance. And just as Branson revolutionized travel across the Atlantic, so Vijay would offer low-cost but fashionable services to a new generation of travellers.

This was all very well, but somehow I always had difficulty in putting the phrases 'Vijay Mallya' and 'low-cost' into the same sentence. There is nothing low-cost about Vijay and I could not see how any extension of the Kingfisher brand could enter a budget segment without damaging the brand image.

My doubts were confirmed when Vijay began announcing his plans for the airline. Every seat would have a video screen. The airhostesses would all look like models. Four different designers would plan the interiors. Another set of designers would do the hostesses' uniforms, and so on.

Now, Vijay professes irritation at the Branson parallels. 'I can't understand how this started. I don't want to be Richard Branson. I want to be Vijay Mallya.' He denies also that Kingfisher was planned as a budget carrier. 'Look at me,' he booms. 'Can you see me starting a budget airline?'

My point, exactly

It is too early to say how well Kingfisher will do. But Vijay has already demonstrated a shrewdness of touch by linking up with

Indian Airlines for infrastructural services and he insists that despite the plethora of services, he is following a model that allows for higher margins on lower costs. My guess is that he has made a mistake by choosing an all-economy format. Given his own image (he is a brand ambassador for Kingfisher, remember?) he could have successfully launched a premium club class and made the kind of profits that Branson makes from Virgin Upper Class. But no doubt, Vijay's people have crunched the numbers and know what they are doing.

When Virgin Atlantic took off, Branson sold off the music business that had first made him rich. Even if Kingfisher does become a huge success, I don't think Vijay will part with the booze business that is the bedrock of his fortune. He has restructured his liquor companies and sold equity to such partners as South African Breweries (another round of restructuring to merge Shaw Wallace brands into United Spirits is currently in progress). But he is still a booze baron at heart.

Just how big a booze baron he is, can be underestimated. After he bought out Shaw Wallace's liquor interests (two decades after he first tried to take over the company), his group is now the world's second-largest liquor manufacturer after Diaego, the British-European conglomerate, which is itself the product of acquisitions and mergers.

His father would, I think, have been proud of him. His style is very different from Vittal's but he has grown the empire to a level that nobody could ever have thought possible. And, he has done it in his own way, not giving a damn about what anybody says.

After all these years, the son has finally proved that he deserves his father's approval.

'Despite being a new party, we still did very well. Maybe, we will do even better in the next election.'

ratan tata

Chairman, Tata Group

▲

So, Ratan Tata is going to stay on as head of the Tata empire till 2012. That, at least, is the way the media have reported the story. And certainly, there's no doubt that Tata Sons has gone back to its old policy of requiring company chairmen to retire at seventy-five and not at seventy.

Except that Ratan Tata himself is not at all sure that he's going to stay in the job for that long. 'I see colleagues, people who have been chairmen of companies, who act as though their lives are over when they step down. I always say to them "have a life of your own, outside of the office",' he explains.

'I am actually quite looking forward to the opportunity to do other things; to take a break from having to work morning and evening.' So, is it possible that he'll step down before he has to?

'Oh yes, it is quite possible.'

How does he feel about the change in the retirement rule, one that many people believe, was made only to benefit him? He's slightly offended by the suggestion that, having instituted a retirement policy to rid the Tata group of the great satraps of the JRD-era, he's quietly changed the rule to ensure his own continuance. First of all, he says, the retirement age was

[
'Yes, I think I am lonely. And what's worse, I'm too diffident to do anything about it.'
]

seventy-five when the satraps departed – it was changed to seventy much later. Secondly, it wasn't his idea. It was a major Tata company (which he refuses to name but which we all know is Tata Steel) that first asked Tata Sons to review the retirement policy for the group. And when the discussion took place, he left the room, aware that he could be regarded as an interested party. So, he played no part in the final decision. There is a tinge of indignation in the tone but you have to strain to catch it. For most of the hour we spend in the Presidential Suite of Delhi's Taj Mahal Hotel (Ratan is, of course, chairman of Taj group), he is remarkably relaxed, willing to answer any question, unperturbed by criticism and eager to talk about the controversies that dogged the early part of his tenure as head of the Tatas.

Some of this confidence stems from the fact that he has pulled off what nobody ever thought he could. He's turned around all the major Tata companies, the group has never been in better financial shape, the international acquisitions continue apace and he's now the darling of the global media. (He was on the cover of *Newsweek*, 4 July 2005.) Plus there's the satisfaction of knowing that his is a very Tata success. He's never deviated from the path of ethics and honesty taught to him by his father Naval and by J.R.D. Tata, his predecessor as head of Tatas.

But most of all, the willingness to talk honestly seems to come from deep within him. He is not an evasive guy. Ask him a straight question and he'll give you a straight answer.

I prefer a young successor

Just suppose, I ask him, that the retirement age had not been extended. He would have stepped down in a couple of years. Had he found a successor?

No, he says candidly, there was no obvious candidate. He had spent a long time looking for a successor but he had achieved only 60 to 70 per cent success. One good thing about the extra time is that he now has the breathing space he needs to find the right successor – and yes, he repeats, he isn't necessarily going to wait till 2012.

What qualities is he looking for in his successor? Is there a job description?

'Some qualities are pretty self-evident,' he says. 'The new man must believe in Tata values, he must demonstrate managerial ability and he must have the vision to run the Tata group.'

But there are other less obvious qualities. Ratan believes that he hasn't been able to complete the task of restructuring the group. He thinks more needs to be done to motivate Tata employees. Any new chairman of Tata Sons will have to be a man with the ability to finish the job.

He's looking, he says, for a younger person. Ideally, he would want a man in his 40s. If no such candidate appears then he would be okay with somebody in his early 50s. But he wants a boss who can stay at the helm long enough to remould and restructure the group.

Does that mean that the next chairman will not be in his late 50s or early 60s as many of the existing candidates are? Ratan is clear. A transitional chairman is an option. But he'd much prefer a young person who could lead the group for a long time. That probably means that all the speculation in the business press about likely successors will now have to go out of the window as the search narrows in on a new generation.

I never thought I'd succeed JRD

Any questions about the Tata succession must inevitably take us back to that day in 1981 when J.R.D. Tata announced that Ratan Tata would be the new chairman of Tata Industries. Was he surprised by the decision? Well, perhaps he was, he says, but he never for a moment thought that chairing Tata Industries meant that he would succeed J.R.D. Tata as the big boss.

Come on, I say, everybody treated the Tata Industries announcement as proof that the succession was a done deal. 'The media certainly treated it that way,' he says, 'but within Tatas, nobody was sure that I would be the successor. And while JRD would say things like "one day you will have to look after the group", he never actually made a firm commitment to me.'

Does that mean that for the full decade that he chaired Tata Industries but not Tata Sons, he lived with the knowledge that he might end up working for somebody else? Yes, that apparently, is exactly how he felt. Who, I ask, could have succeeded JRD?

'Nani Palkhivala,' he says, ' Nani was a very strong contender. It was only because he became such a vocal critic of the government that JRD thought his political views might have become a liability to the Tatas.'

Who else?

'Rusi Mody,' he replies. ' In fact, for most of the 1980s, I personally thought that Rusi was certain to be the next head of Tatas. He ran Tata Steel very successfully, had a larger-than-life personality and Jeh (JRD) was very fond of him. I think Jeh liked him because he had many of the qualities that Jeh would have liked to have had himself. Rusi was gregarious. He was outgoing. He could go into a crowd of workers and charm them.'

He offers as an example of J.R.D. Tata's faith in Rusi Mody. The proposal – in the late 1980s – for Rusi to take over Telco as well as Tisco. ' But then of course, Rusi put his foot in his mouth.'

I tell him I have heard the story – from Rusi himself. Apparently, just as they were preparing to announce that Rusi would take over Telco, irresponsible journalists quoted Rusi as saying that Sumant Moolgavkar had run Telco very badly. Moolgavkar lost his temper and refused to let Rusi succeed him even though Rusi explained that the quotes had been fabricated.

'Yes,' says Ratan tactfully, ' Rusi did claim later that he had been misquoted.'

The turnaround story

Any discussion about Rusi Mody leads us to the two charges most frequently levelled against Ratan Tata in the 1990s. One: that he was a hopeless businessman who had got the job only because of his surname.

And two: that he was so insecure about his own limited abilities that he quickly got rid of the satraps on whom JRD had depended. 'Well, let me say first of all that I was never insecure about anybody else or their position in the group,' he says coolly. 'But I am a sensitive person and when people like Rusi Mody started saying these hurtful things about me, I took it very badly. I had always looked up to Rusi, especially when I was in Jamshedpur, and I felt very hurt that he should direct so much of his anger my way. It was emotionally very wrenching.'

Let's do this step by step, I suggest. Was he really the business dum-dum that his critics would claim? Was it true that he ran Nelco to the ground? That he forced the Tata textile business into liquidation?

It is not the sort of question people usually ask Ratan Tata to his face but he is remarkably unperturbed. In fact, he seems eager to set the record straight.

He starts with Nelco, long regarded as an albatross around his neck.

'When I took charge of the company, we had 2 per cent market share of the consumer electronics market. Our losses were 40 per cent of turnover. I was able to turn that around so that we had 20 per cent market share of consumer electronics and had diversified into new areas including professional electronics, inverters, computers etc. And by the end, we actually made a profit and declared a dividend.'

It is not his claim, he says, that Nelco was ever a huge success but surely he can take some credit for turning it around? And, he adds, if the Tatas had been willing to invest in the company, things could have been much better.

As for the textile experience, he was given Empress Mill when it was a sick unit. He made it profitable and declared a dividend. Then, J.R.D. Tata asked him to look after the Central India Mill. 'At around this time, the whole Indian textile industry went through a bad patch. So, some Tata directors, chiefly Nani Palkhivala, took the line that we should liquidate the mill. I argued with them. We needed just Rs 50 lakhs to turn it around. But Nani opposed giving us the money and we closed the mill down.'

Then, Ratan Tata shows a little emotion. 'I was so disgusted by that decision that when I got my annual bonus from the Tatas, I gave it to the officers of the company. These were perfectly blameless people who now had lost their jobs through no fault of theirs because of a bad corporate decision. They had homes to run and children to educate.'

It is not a side of Ratan Tata that he allows us to see very often.

The biggest regret in my life

What about the satraps, I ask. Inevitably, the conversation turns to Rusi Mody again. It is hard to escape the feeling that of all the relationships that have gone wrong in Ratan Tata's professional life, it is the break with Mody that has wounded him the most.

'I still don't understand why Rusi behaved the way he did. He was my friend. He was Jeh's favourite. But he just became totally unreasonable. I remember one board meeting where we asked him why he kept giving interviews running down Tata Steel, of which he was the chairman. (By then, J.J. Irani was MD.) He just got up and said, "I will leave the room because this subject has been raised." And then, to our astonishment, the chairman of Tata Steel got up and walked out of his own board meeting. After that he didn't turn up for board meetings and kept bad-mouthing the company. Finally, the board had to remove him.'

He seems genuinely bemused. 'I think he did himself a disservice. And I think his behaviour harmed Aditya Kashyap, who was a very intelligent and capable executive but who felt he had to support Rusi.'

Does he regret some of the bitterness that permeated the Tata group during that era? Yes, he says, he clearly does.

106

But his biggest regret has nothing to do with the satraps. It has to do with J.R.D. Tata himself. 'For the last six years or so of his life, we were very close,' he recalls, 'but I really regret that we did not become closer earlier. That is probably the biggest regret of my life.'

And the loneliest moments

Since he seems in such a candid mood, I ask about his own success and failures. Given that for the first five or six years of his time as head of Tatas, so many people wrote him off, were there lonely moments?

'Oh, yes,' he says, 'there were many lonely moments. There were many moments when I felt alone, frustrated and despondent.' He talks about the phase when Telco lost Rs 600 crore and the critics decided that Ratan was simply not up to the job: 'I tried to explain to people that our market share was still the same. It was the industry that was going through a bad phase. But nobody would believe me. Then, when the market revived, Telco began making profits again. Once again, I tried to explain that it wasn't that we'd turned the company around. We still had the same market share as always. But market trends had changed. Even then,' he laughs, 'people wouldn't believe me.'

Then, there was the terrible and bloody labour dispute involving Rajan Nair weeks after Ratan had taken over Telco. 'It was a terrible time,' he recalls. 'There was violence. There were stabbings. The police appeared to be on Rajan Nair's side. And there was absolutely nobody in Poona (Pune now) who was willing to come out openly in favour of us except for old Dr Kalyani (father of Baba Kalyani), whose support I will never ever forget,' he remembers. 'But if Telco hadn't fought that battle and if we hadn't won, Rajan Nair would have ruled Pune.'

So, that was a lonely time? 'Oh yes, it was a terrible time.' And of course, there's the story of the Indica, the car that everybody regarded as Ratan's folly but which became the great success of

Tata Motors. 'I always thought we should build a small car,' he says. 'But all small or medium-sized foreign cars are meant to be self-driven which means that nobody pays any attention to the back seat which sort of sinks down when you sit in it. I wanted a car that could be chauffer-driven, where the back wasn't too low – really. I wanted to build a modern version of the Ambassador at a competitive price.'

As the process of making the car got underway, many of Ratan's critics thought it would be his undoing. 'Even within Tatas, people kept asking me to distance myself from the project so that when it failed I wouldn't be stuck with the blame. And when I refused to do that, they distanced themselves from me.' He smiles. 'But it was a good thing in retrospect, because I got very involved with the team and we worked very closely together and were much more motivated as a result.'

It was destiny, not the surname

I ask him about the manner in which he is perceived by his colleagues, and by the public at large. Because the bulk of Tata Sons is now owned by various charities, the Tatas themselves are not multi-billionaires. But it does not follow that they are not rich either. As Ratan concedes, 'I do have capital of my own.'

In the old days, when his beloved grandmother was alive, the Tatas were among the richest people in Bombay (Mumbai now). Ratan himself grew up in astonishing luxury at a huge villa in the centre of Bombay (bits of which later became Sterling Cinema and Deutsche Bank).

And yet, if you look at his lifestyle now, he lives like any professional manager – actually, all the top corporate honchos I know, have lifestyles vastly in excess of Ratan's. He's lived for years in the same flat (from before he became chairman of Tatas) in Bakhtawar in Colaba and the few people who've been to his house say that it is the home of a bachelor who loves reading and dogs; certainly not the home of the head of India's largest conglomerate. Even J.R.D. Tata, who was not exactly ostentatious, lived in far greater luxury – in a very nice Cumbala Hill bungalow – far better than Ratan does now.

Could it be, I ask, that personal wealth doesn't matter so much to him? And isn't that odd for somebody who was brought up as a rich boy? 'Yes, I did grow up amidst a lot of wealth,' he concedes. 'But don't forget that I spent ten years in America trying to live on the Reserve Bank's allowances (the Tatas would, of course, never buy dollars on the black market) and the money was never enough. So I had to take all kinds of jobs, including washing dishes, to make ends meet. That sort of thing helps you forget that your family is rich quite quickly.'

And now? He's added hundreds of millions of dollars in value to the Tata empire. Does he mind that virtually none of it has come to him? 'Oh, no. It is not something I even think about.' The other popular view of Ratan is that he's painfully shy, almost a recluse. 'That's true,' he says.

But, I persist, I think it goes deeper than that. I think he's also, at core, a very lonely man.

He pauses. 'That's fair,' he says finally. 'Yes, I think I am lonely. And what's worse, I'm too diffident to do anything about it.'

He went away to America to study architecture when he was young. And yet, here he is, running a huge business. Is this something he would have liked to do? Or is he just a prisoner to his surname? 'I think I would have remained an architect, regardless of my surname,' he responds. 'I was called Tata when I decided not to go into business and become an architect. But then, my grandmother, to whom I was very attached, fell very ill and I had to keep coming back to India to see her. And after a while, after I had been here so many times, one thing led to another and I just never went back.'

So, in the end, it wasn't the surname that trapped him. It was his destiny that finally caught up with him?

Ratan Tata pauses a while and then, he smiles. 'Yes, I think you can say that.'

chronology

All profiles were first published in the *Hindustan Times,* Mumbai edition under the *HT* Leadership Series:

Ratan Tata, 24 July 2005
Nusli Wadia, 25 July 2005
Rajeev Chandrasekhar, 1 August 2005
Nandan Nilekani, 8 August 2005
Subhash Chandra, 15 August 2005
Azim Premji, 22 August 2005
Kumar Mangalam Birla, 29 August 2005
Uday Kotak, 5 September 2005
Sunil Bharati Mittal, 19 September 2005
Vijay Mallya, 26 September 2005
Bikki Oberoi, 29 January 2006